AuthorHouse™
1663 Liberty Drive
Bloomington, IN 47403
www.authorhouse.com
Phone: 1 (800) 839-8640

Published by AuthorHouse   03/06/2017

ISBN: 978-1-5246-7366-6 (sc)
ISBN: 978-1-5246-7368-0 (hc)
ISBN: 978-1-5246-7367-3 (e)

Library of Congress Control Number: 2017903057

Print information available on the last page.

This book is printed on acid-free paper.

Cover photo: Jeff Preston, 2016 View from Van Sickle State Park

57 DOG-FRIENDLY TRAILS

in California's Foothills and the Sierra Nevada

DEBBI PRESTON

authorHOUSE®

ABOUT THE AUTHOR

Debbi Preston previously authored 48 Dog-Friendly Trails and Dog-Friendly Trails for All Seasons. Her inspiration to explore local trails came from her dog, Toots. After losing Toots to cancer, Preston found the trails less enjoyable and was inspired to write "Tails" from the Trails to honor Toots' legacy. Eventually, the Preston family welcomed their new Australian shepherd puppy, Maggie, and started sharing the trails with her.

Preston shared her favorite trails with Maggie and together they discovered new places and different ways to reach old destinations. Aware that the old guidebooks needed updating after several seasons with fires and flooding negatively affecting some trails, and with fees and parking changes, Preston decided to create 57 Dog-Friendly Trails in California's Foothills and the Sierra Nevada, incorporating her favorite trails along with all of the new ones she had discovered.

"Since publishing my first two guidebooks, I have taken adventure trips to hike in New Zealand, Iceland, and the Galapagos – all great destinations. I can honestly say, however, that in my fourteen years hiking, our local trails match those I visited in these other countries. I am happy to share my favorite trails in this new book."

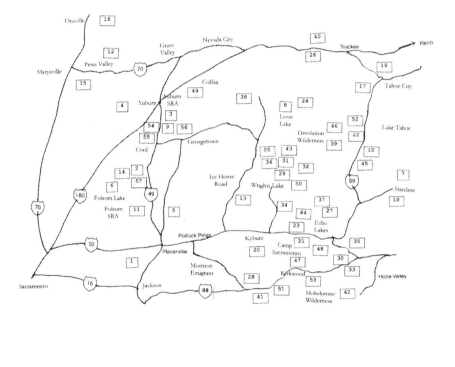

TABLE OF CONTENTS

JUNE

JULY

AUGUST

SEPTEMBER

October

November

December

INTRODUCTION

Trails change! This is the most important thing to remember. Parking areas change, fees change, old markers vanish, and new trails emerge. Since publishing *48 Dog-Friendly Trails* and *Dog-Friendly Trails for All Seasons*, many changes have occurred, necessitating this revised guidebook. This book contains our favorite trails, the trails we like visiting multiple times each year. There are also new trails, new ways to access old destinations, and new parking directions for some trailheads. We lost some great trails as well. Fire destroyed the Hunters Trail area, and storms changed Tamaroo Bar (Robie Point Trail), moving all of the sand to the other side of the river making the beach inaccessible. Fortunately, we found some great new trails to replace our old favorites.

Seasons change! A trail accessible one year in November may be covered in snow the next year and not reachable until late spring. A trail can open early or it can open later in the year. While trails are placed in appropriate months, realize that a late or early snow could change the month you should plan to visit. Resources are listed at the back of this book with phone numbers to call with any questions about the conditions for a particular hike.

Hiking requires common sense and the acceptance of its many risks. It is essential that you carry a good map and perhaps a pedometer to mark your mileage. Then, if a sign has changed or is missing, you can still refer to the trail description of distances, and to your trail map, to verify your path choice.

Do not attempt a trail too difficult for your abilities, unless you are willing to turn around once out of your comfort zone. Allow plenty of time for your hike, and turn back if you cannot complete the journey before dark. Most importantly, be safe and enjoy.

Hiking is a pleasurable experience any one can partake in, regardless of age or physical abilities. You can adapt any of these trails to meet your particular needs. Always be mindful of safety for everyone in your group, never exceeding the weakest member's capabilities. The point is to have fun, enjoy an outdoor experience, and get some exercise. Hiking provides mental, physical, and social stimuli to help keep you healthy, strong, and youthful.

Dog-Friendly Trails

All of the trails in this book are accessible to dogs (some have leash requirements). On some trails, you may encounter joggers, mountain bikers, horses, or other pack animals. If you bring your dog, be sure it will be comfortable sharing the trail. You need to know if your dog will react correctly if you come across a snake or bear on your route. The trail is not a good place for an aggressive dog, so be sure your dog is socialized properly. If at all questionable, plan to leash your dog for the best control.

In order to continue having trails open to dogs, we must all be sure to follow leash rules, and to pick up after our own dog, and others, to keep trails clean. Do not give other hikers the opportunity to complain about dogs on a trail.

A dog on the trail with you is a great asset for helping to protect and guide you. They have great instincts and can really improve your outing. In addition to it providing great exercise and socializing, hiking trails are beneficial for dogs as well as people by providing a cooler habitat. A dog's first means of cooling itself is through its paws (panting is the secondary means). Walking in the summer on hot asphalt or cement is not good for your animal; the dirt mountain trails, the many streams and lakes to step into, and the cooler air at the higher elevations all combine to provide a much healthier summer situation.

The trails also give a dog the opportunity to explore new areas, using instincts to smell and listen to discover what the outdoors present. Hiking gives dogs the opportunity to run and socialize with other dogs and humans. The outdoors provides your dog with places to dig, to find sticks, rocks, and bones to chew on, and the chance to work by carrying its own daypack with treats (never exceed 30% of your dog's weight in its pack) or pull you up a hill by the leash. Trails provide a multitude of experiences and remove the boredom of a typical day home alone.

Start exercising your dog slowly if it has been a couch potato. If you have a puppy, do not do trails with large rocks to jump down from until their bones and joints are more developed. Ask your puppy's veterinarian about when you can safely introduce the more rugged trails into your routine. A well-exercised dog is a happier, healthier, and less destructive dog.

People-Friendly Trails

Moreover, all of these trails are what I consider as people-friendly as well. Hiking is great for improving muscle tone, joints, weight, and balance. There are great cognitive benefits to hiking with encountering new circumstances, trail reading challenges, and studying the history or nature of a location. As you rock hop, or walk across a log to ford a stream, you are challenging your brain. In addition to the physical benefits, there are great social ones as well. Exploring new places boosts your confidence, and this increased sense of "I can do it" spills over into your daily life.

What makes a trail people-friendly? First, it is the feeling of safety. A trail must allow dogs in order to be people-friendly. A dog provides safety, protecting you from other humans and making you aware of any wild animals in the area. A dog has such a good sense of smell that it can more easily find a trail or a water source than you can. In an extreme emergency, a dog can also provide you with warmth. Above all, a dog makes a great hiking companion, committing you to exercising.

In order to be included in this book, trails not only had to allow dogs, but also needed to be free of unnecessary risks, such as scaling rocks, or extremely narrow paths along steep drop-offs. If a trail is dangerous physically, then it did not make this book.

I want you to feel safe on the trail, as well as with leaving your car behind unprotected. Of course, you should never leave any valuables in your car to invite a break-in, but a trailhead away from large populations is safer than one closer to high-traffic roads. Never leave any food items in your car, including sodas or gum, to protect yourself from bear break-ins. If a bear sees a cooler in your car or can smell any food, there is a chance of damage to your vehicle. A cooler with water only, hidden from sight, should be all right.

Second, after safety concerns, for a trail to be people-friendly, there needs to be a visual reward, either at the destination (such as the hike to Ralston Peak), or along the journey (like the hike to Scotts Lake). Nature is abundant with beauty, and by hiking some of these trails, you get to enjoy its many wonders. There are many photo opportunities along these trails, as well as discoveries of romantic spots for lingering. These trails are not just physical challenges, but places to discover beauty, take family members, and find inner peace.

Finally, minimal fees are associated with these trails, and many offer free parking, making them great places to take new friends. Every month, there is an easy option to share with someone new to hiking. You can plan a picnic along a scenic part of a trail and just enjoy the outdoors with a friend. There is no requirement to go any further on a trail than you care to.

Gear: Most important for you is to have a good pair of hiking boots with good tread. Secondly, have a daypack pre-loaded with hiking supplies. At a minimum, it should always contain a first aid kit, pedometer, pocketknife, whistle, matches and flint, money, toilet paper (or wet wipes), shovel, sunscreen, insect repellant, and a plastic bag for scooping your dog's waste if burying is not an option. Keep your fishing license and gear in your bag.

On the day of the hike, add plenty of fresh water for you and your dog, and a bowl or other device for you dog to use. While it will be generally safe for your dog to drink from lakes and streams, humans can get very sick from Giardia lambia (an organism passed from human to human). So pack more than enough water for yourself and avoid being tempted from drinking nature's water, possibly contaminated by other humans. (Dehydration is worse than possible water parasites, so in an emergency drink available running water. If it is contaminated, you will not have a reaction until you get home). Please do everything you can to avoid adding to human contamination and relieve yourself far from any water sources. Use your shovel to bury both yours and your dog's waste 6" deep and 200' away from water sources, trails, or campsites.

Also, pack plenty of snacks (more than you expect to eat), and an extra clothing layer for unexpected weather changes. Remember, there is no such thing as a bad day for hiking, just bad gear. Bring along a leash for your dog, and a hat, sunglasses, watch, phone, and camera for you. See if you can, download a trail/mapping app to your phone. Carry $10.00 for parking fees (a $5.00 and five $1.00 bills is the best combination). You may find trekking poles useful to help with steep climbs and balance, especially at log crossings. Finally, pack a map of the area you will be covering, and this trail book with the trail description.

Safety: After packing your items, make sure you tell someone where you will be going and when you expect to return. When you do return, let that person know you are back safely. This is important whether you are traveling alone or with others – let someone not going with you know your itinerary in case there is any emergency.

Carefully plan your trip ahead of time to make sure you can complete your trip before dusk. Be willing to turn around and head back if darkness or thunderstorms threaten. If you encounter raging waters to cross or heavy snow patches hiding the trail, do not try to continue. End your hike and wait a few weeks to try this trail again. If you lose sight of the next trail marker, or in any way cannot clearly see the trail, then stop, retrace your steps to the last known certain point on the trail, and look ahead for the next sign. If unsure, then do not proceed. Stay on the trail to avoid getting lost or injured. If injured while on a trail, it is much more likely that help will come than if you were off-trail.

Dangers: Following the safety advice, you should be able to avoid getting lost or injured. Other dangers to consider are the animals and insects you might encounter. The animals that most people fear are rattlesnakes, bears, and mountain lions. If you encounter a snake on the trail, stop and let the snake get out of the way. A snake wants to avoid you if possible. Allow it to do so by keeping your dog from pestering it and giving it adequate space to leave. People and dogs usually are bitten when trying to handle or harm a snake. The higher in elevation that you go, the less likely you will be to encounter a rattlesnake; however, they can be found as high as 9,000'.

Similarly, a bear wants to avoid humans (unless you are backpacking and have food available). If you see a bear, stop and let it move out of the area. Do not try to approach or scare it away. I learned the "stop and wait method" from my instinctive dog, Toots. It worked with both a snake and a bear we encountered while hiking. Fortunately, we have never encountered a mountain lion. Based on what I have read, the rules regarding this animal are, first, **do not run**. Stand your ground and look as big as possible. Raise your arms and open a jacket to look larger. Climb onto a large rock or log to seem taller. Do not bend over, but do try to access a stick or weapon of some sort (your trekking poles would work great). If you have children, pick them up so they do not panic and run – no matter how awkward, pick them up without bending or crouching. Make noise, speaking firmly and loudly, and try to scare the animal off. The object is to do everything that you can to prove you are not prey and that you could pose a danger to it.

Do not hit the trails before it is clearly daylight, and be back to your car before dusk to minimize the chance of encountering a mountain lion. Keep aware of your surroundings and do not block out noise with earphones. If you jog, you need to be especially careful, since your movements mimic prey. Be sure to take a dog along for your run; try not to jog alone, and if there are any small children, keep them in front of you.

The most likely animal encounter you may suffer is that of mosquitoes and ticks. Use insect repellant liberally before and during your hike to ward off mosquitoes and other biting insects. Staying on the trail is the best way to avoid ticks, prevalent in the grassy foothills. Check yourself to see if any ticks are crawling on you. It is easiest to spot them if you wear light-colored clothing on your spring hikes, with long sleeves and full-length pants. Try to remove any ticks before they attach to you. Ticks carry the very harmful Lyme disease and Rocky Mountain Spotted Fever, and both can make you quite sick. If one becomes attached, pull it straight out, holding as much of the body as close to your skin as possible. You can use tweezers, if available, or your fingers. Be sure to treat your dog ahead of time with a tick collar or monthly tick treatments, and on the trail use repellant as you would for yourself. If you are fearful of using conventional repellants, try using some essential oils and combine 20 drops of Purification, 5 drops of Lavender, and a 2 drops of Peppermint in a 16 oz bottle of distilled water. Spray the mixture hourly, massaging into the dog's coat. Other oils can be useful to soothe a sting, cut, or muscle injury, and even to provide a healthier sunscreen option.

Other than animals and insects, the other danger is with plants, most notably with poison oak. In addition to poison oak, some thistles and burr-carrying plants can cause problems. Learn how to recognize poison oak and its three-leaf configuration so you can avoid it. If you do accidentally touch it, immediately try to wash the affected area in cool water. Do not handle clothing that has contacted the plant unless you can immediately wash your hands afterwards. Even in the winter when the poison oak leaves are absent, the plant can still cause a severe rash. While poison oak may not bother your dog, the oil can transfer from your pooch to you, causing an allergic reaction.

Snowshoeing: The mountain hiking season is from mid-June to mid-November in most years. To extend this five-month season, consider taking up snowshoeing. You can order a pair of snowshoes from a catalog based on your weight and head out for the trails, or you can take advantage of programs allowing you to try out some gear and get instruction before purchasing any equipment. Consider getting some good trekking poles for better stability and more of an upper body workout.

With snowshoeing, remember you are at a high altitude so the air is thinner. That, plus the higher difficulty level of traversing through snow, makes any outing more aerobic than a typical hike. You should plan for shorter routes when shoeing, since you cannot travel as many miles per hour as when hiking, and remember that winter days are shorter as well.

Your clothing must include many layers so you can be ready for any weather condition. A hat and gloves are essential, as is waterproofing your boots. Remember that the snow intensifies the sun and you can easily be sunburned, so apply sunscreen liberally. Put a spare pair of socks in your pack (packed in a waterproof bag), and a dry pair of shoes and socks in your car to change into on your return. Denim is not a good clothing choice for the snow since it does not dry easily if you fall and get wet. Instead, use snow pants or hiking pants made of a quick-drying material.

Be aware of your dog's needs in the snow as well, considering such items as shoes or musher's cream (musherssecret.net) for their paws. Not all dogs will be sensitive and need shoes, but all dogs should have their paws checked periodically for ice buildup on pads and the fur between the toes. Make sure they drink plenty of water on your outing as well. Consider a piece of warm clothing for your more sensitive shorthaired pooch. Start with a simple walk in the snow to see if it is a good environment for your particular pet.

Snowshoe etiquette is to stay out of cross-country skier's tracks. Stay on marked trails to avoid getting lost or creating any avalanche conditions. Trails are usually marked with blue diamonds high on trees, or ribbons on lower branches. As with all trails, if you do not clearly see the next marker or a clear track, do not continue forward.

Photography: If you love photography, then you will love hiking and discovering new sites to capture. With the popularity of camera phones and digital cameras, you gain the opportunity to take many more pictures than you would with film cameras. Take advantage of this, and do not skip a great flower picture in hopes of seeing a better display further on in the hike. The problem with this is twofold: you may not see a better display after all; and, on your return trip, you may not see the original object again. Things look different on the return trip, sun light changes, new items stand out, and previous ones lose focus. Take camera shots as they come.

Trail Routes

Selection: Plan your hike by first reading the complete trail description to make sure it suits everyone in your group. Study any topographical map if available to see if there are any extremely steep portions on the trail. A topographic map uses contour lines to show 40' elevation changes. The denser the lines are, the steeper the grade. Also, look at the trail difficulty rating to help determine if it is a suitable choice.

I rate trails from '1' (easiest) to '5' (most difficult), based on a combination of length, elevation gain, and trail reading difficulty. This is a subjective coding, but should be useful in helping you to determine a hike's suitability for your group.

Etiquette: Always keep your dog in your control and follow all leashing requirements. All of these trails are dog friendly, but you cannot just let your animal run loose and out of control. Do not let your dog disturb any wild animals, and control them around any pack and saddle animals. Always be considerate and do not leave any dog waste on the trail for others to contend with. Yield to uphill hikers or backpackers with a heavy pack and to all trail animals such as horses, llamas, and goats among others. When yielding, step off the trail but stay in view of the oncoming animals. You can spook an animal if you are behind a bush or tree because you appear more predatory. Let the pack animal have the uphill position while you stay on the lower side of the trail.

Reading the trail: Most of the foothill trails have an obvious dirt path for you to follow easily. The mountain trails, however, prove more difficult at times, especially when you cross over large sections of rock slabs. In these cases, without a trail and footsteps to follow, you need to look for manmade markings to find your way. Typical markings consist of "ducks", blazes, ribbons, and diamond markers. The use of "ducks" is prevalent in Desolation and Mokelumne Wilderness. These are piles of three small rocks conspicuously placed on larger rocks with the larger bottom one resembling a duck's body, the middle one the neck, and the smaller one on top for the head. When you cannot follow footsteps, you need to look ahead on the trail to the next rock pile to stay on course. A very tall pile of rocks is called a 'cairn' and rarer in the wilderness. A blaze is usually a manmade cut in a tree's bark above eye-level. Less frequently, you may find ribbons used to mark either snowshoe or spur trails. Most snowshoe routes are marked with blue or orange diamonds high on tree trunks, and ribbons on branches. Do beware, however, that sometimes a well-meaning hiker may place a new marker and not be necessarily on trail.

Along with the various markings, there often are posts or other signage to indicate a major trail junction. Along with a good map and trail description, you should be able to read the signs of the trail and safely make it to your destination and back. Always be mindful when you reach a lake to look backwards at your route in so you can easily find it again when you are ready to depart. Do not rely solely on a GPS device as service could be lost, or even the device itself, and you could find yourself in trouble. Think of devices as a backup plan, not your primary source of direction. Pay attention to trail markers, such as a dead tree, a large rock, or a grouping of objects. You can look for these on your return trip to help you stay on the correct path.

If you hike alone, then you have to take all these precautions even more seriously to avoid any chance of getting lost or injured. Overall, you want to have a safe and enjoyable experience. By having your dog join you on your adventure, you will have their great sense of direction to help to guide you as well.

Wilderness Permits: Entrance into Desolation Wilderness requires a day-use permit. These permits are free, and are usually available at trailheads during the prime hiking season from July 1 through September 30. In the off-season, you can obtain a permit at either the Mill Run or the Tahoe Ranger Station. On Highway 50 in Fresh Pond, you take the Mill Run exit to reach the Pacific Ranger District and obtain a permit. They do not need to be open for you to get the permit, since they have a supply in a box outside of their offices. The Lake Tahoe Visitor Center is 3.2 miles on Highway 89 after the 89/50 split in South Lake Tahoe. Permits are not currently required for the Mokelumne Wilderness.

Damage: I want everyone to enjoy nature on these trails, but if you plan to leave litter behind, please stay home. There is never an excuse to litter. Be prepared to take home everything you bring with you, and carry a spare plastic bag to pick up any items you find along the way. If there are garbage facilities at the trailhead or any picnic areas, please still pack out your garbage so these receptacles do not fill. Garbage left at trails attracts flies, bees, and possibly other scavengers. It also spoils the overall beauty of the outdoors. Remember the Forest Service motto, "Leaving Only Footprints and Taking Only Memories."

Leave no other reminders of your visit either. Remember always to stay on established trails. Do not create your own shortcuts or switchbacks. Unnecessary minor trails are an eyesore for future hikers. Further, you can seriously damage fragile wildflowers any time you leave the trail. It takes years for some of these flowers to re-establish due to your lack of consideration. Never pick the flowers or in any way destroy nature's wonders. Do not disturb any plant life or in any way leave your mark on the environment. I encourage exploring spur trails throughout the book, but these are existing side trails – never make new cuts off trail.

Hiking with a dog: There are responsibilities associated with taking your dog on the trails. If you are not certain to find water plentiful on your hike, then be sure to carry some for your pooch and have a means of providing a container for easy drinking. Know your dog's capabilities and do not exceed them. If he is older, has shorter legs, or has been a couch potato, do not expect him to travel at a fast pace. The point of the journey is to have a good time. If your dog shows signs of fatigue, then stop and rest, and consider turning back.

Always carry a leash, even on trails where a leash is not required. You never know what situation you may encounter when you need to restrain your dog. For instance, you could site a bear in the distance, your dog may be spooked by gunshots, or an approaching dog could give you concern. Always maintain verbal control and be ready to restrain as needed.

Never leave your dog's poop on a trail. Carry a plastic bag for proper disposal, or a shovel for burying it. In an emergency, find a stick and remove it from the trail so another hiker does not accidentally step in it.

Items essential in your pack:
1. First aid kit and pocketknife
2. Map
3. Hat
4. Ample water for you and for your dog
5. Ample food, enough for an extra day if needed
6. Whistle and flashlight (with extra batteries)
7. Insect repellant
8. Sun screen
9. Layered clothing
10. Waterproof matches and flint (fires are not allowed in Desolation Wilderness except in the case of an emergency)

Also good to bring along:
1. Sunglasses
2. Camera
3. Trail book/Wildflower book (in season)
4. Watch
5. Walking poles
6. Spare socks
7. Small fold-up shovel and toilet paper
8. Money for parking fees – a $5.00 bill and five $1.00 bills
9. Plastic bag for dog leavings; leash
10. Pedometer

Trail Wisdom and Etiquette:
1. Let someone know where you are going and when you will return.
2. Yield to uphill hikers and to all equestrians and pack animals.
3. Pick up or bury any dog leavings.
4. Do not allow your dog to bother the wildlife or other hikers.
5. When arriving at a lake, always note the trail in, and look for markers to remind you of your path later when you are ready to leave.

6. Do not continue on an unclear trail until you can see your next marker or other sure sign of the trail.
7. Do not attempt a trail above your hiking abilities.
8. Do not rush; always make sure of your footing to avoid injury.
9. Turn back if thunderstorms threaten.
10. Allow plenty of time for your hike to avoid darkness (dusk brings out more wild animals, so be sure to be back to your car well before then).

Get outside and have some fun.

Snow play at Loon Lake

JANUARY

1. El Dorado Trail
2. Cronan Ranch
3. Lake Clementine
4. Hidden Falls

The foothill trails are great in January for a few reasons. In later months, the trails are more crowded, creating limits on an off leash experience. While spring brings some fantastic wildflower displays, rattlesnakes and poison oak also flourish, so winter is a great time to experience these trails.

Cronan Ranch

1 – El Dorado Trail Trestle Segment
Missouri Flat to Forni Road
Placerville, CA

Difficulty:	1
Distance:	3.0 miles (2.7 on the bike trail and 0.3 to Memorial)
Elevation:	Gradual uphill with 100' gain

Directions: Heading east on Highway 50, take Exit 44A for Missouri Flat Road. Turn right (south) from the off-ramp onto Missouri Flat. Continue 0.8 miles on Missouri Flat Road, just beyond Wal-Mart where the two lanes become one, and locate the parking area for the bike trail on your left (adjacent to Sierra Door & Supply). There is room here for about 15 cars to park. If full, do not park in front of Sierra Door & Supply.

Description: This is a great place to start out the New Year with some outdoor activity. If the kids received new bikes for Christmas, a new puppy joined the family, or you finally resolved to get into better physical shape, this is the perfect trail for you and the entire family to begin. Although considered a bike trail, at this time of year you are much more likely to run into fellow hikers and joggers than you are bikers. Nevertheless, always observe the rules of the trail, and walk on the left hand side at all times for better safety.

Starting from the parking area, you can pick up a free doggy waste bag donated by Hangtown Kennel Club (there are numerous trashcans along the trail for depositing any waste). The trail at first competes with local traffic and businesses, but eventually it moves away and becomes more rustic. Numerous exercise stations line the trail for optional activities. There are also benches for resting along the trail that follows along an old railroad path, now paved over for easy passage. Since it was once the path for trains, its uphill grade is gradual, with sweeping curves that would have accommodated a moving train.

At 1.0 miles, you cross over Weber Creek on the old trestle bridge, originally built in 1903, but now modified with heavy planks instead of tracks. Mid-way across the creek, a lookout allows for a 100' view down to the creek. After leaving the creek, you come to a large pasture beside the trail that will be resplendent in wildflowers later in the spring. The air is crisp, with a slight smell of fresh pine. Overhead, hawks soar, and below you hear the sounds of frogs coming from numerous pools of water.

This first section of trail ends at Forni Road, next to the County Jail. From here, you have several options. You can turn around and walk back to your vehicle or take a short walk to a beautiful Veteran's Memorial. Just walk up Forni Road 0.1 mile, and walk left on Ray Lawyer Drive across the Highway 50 overpass toward the county buildings another 0.2 miles. The memorial is on your left at the first building up a flight of 26 stairs. This site is a great place to reflect on our veterans and to support our troops. A third option is to continue on a newer section of the bike path in the direction of Placerville to the Placerville Station. This will connect you with an older section of the trail through shaded portions of the city in the direction of Camino. You could continue another 7.0 miles on this route, while gaining another 1200' in elevation.

Share with: Joggers, bikers, in-line skaters, wheelchairs, and equestrians (limited trailer parking available). This is a truly multi-use trail, suitable for anyone.

2 – Cronan Ranch Trails
Pilot Hill, CA

Difficulty: 3 (or 2 depending on option taken)
Distance: 5.0-mile loop (shorter options are available)
Elevation: 500' gain on described loop

Directions: On Highway 49, coming from Coloma, 5 miles from the bridge crossing the South Fork American River, turn left onto Pedro Hill Road. Coming from Auburn on Highway 49, make a right turn 1.0 mile south of Pilot Hill onto Pedro Hill Road (about 16 miles south of Auburn).

The large trailhead parking area is a short distance from here toward the left. Leave the larger parking spaces for horse trailers and park near the map at the start of the trailhead or along the exit road.

Description: The Cronan Ranch offers trails throughout its 1,418 acres, open to hikers, joggers, mountain bikers, and equestrians. Once private ranch property, it is now public and run by the Bureau of Land Management (BLM). The trails are well marked with signs, and multiple maps at the start of the trail will help you to plan a good route for the day. Do not let the number of cars and horse trailers alarm you as there are numerous trail options, and your fellow outdoor enthusiasts will disperse throughout the ranch.

Starting beyond the parking area, walk up the hill on Ranch Road for .025 mile and reach a kiosk with a map of the trails in the ranch. You can plan your own route or follow my description for a fun loop trail that will take advantage of the various amenities of the park.

At the kiosk, turn left onto the Down and Up Trail. After another 0.5 mile, the trail comes to an intersection – go right here onto the East Ridge Trail (may not be signed). Continue 0.15 miles before reaching the intersection with the Hidden Valley Trail to your right. Stay on the East Ridge Trail and its undulating path. Along this next stretch, two picnic tables provide for a nice respite and a view down to the South

Fork American River. From the first bench, you also have a view down to the old movie site for "Love Comes Softly."

The East Ridge Trail will start a continuous descent after leaving the second picnic area, taking you down to the river. Along the river, you will have many access spots via spur trails down to the water. A couple of nice beaches and coves are available for your lunch spot and a swim for your dog. Numerous upgraded toilet facilities line the trail along the river.

Water levels fluctuate on the river suddenly with frequent water releases for kayakers. My friends visited here and for their lunch break at the river did some rock hopping out to a little island. Within a half hour, the water had risen, making a rock hop back to shore impossible. It was a dangerous walk through the water and they had to rescue their dog when the river swept it away. Never leave you dog unattended and stay aware of the water levels.

For the trip back, return to the "main" trail from your picnic spot and continue to walk downstream. Just before reaching the third toilet building, locate a dirt road leading uphill. Take this road and wind uphill, staying to your left until you reach the "Love Comes Softly" movie site on your right. Most of the site is now in ruins, and you can no longer go inside of the original cabin. There is a picnic table here for a short break in the shade. From here, locate the trail marked "Long Valley Trail" and take this route to return to the parking area.

Another more strenuous option for your return from the river is to return to the "main" trail and turn right instead to start the loop back. At the start, you are returning on the same trail on which you arrived, but after passing through a break in fencing marked with a '5', take the trail to your right. (The East Ridge Trail is the one on your left.) For the longer, and tougher, option, continue ahead past this point, now on the aptly named Down & Up Trail.

You will make some 200-foot "ups and downs" along the oak-shaded trail before coming to a small stream lined with blackberries. This is a nice resting spot before continuing again uphill. This next stretch is tough, with a 400-foot elevation gain. Avoid any turns you see along the way, staying straight to the top of the hill. Near the top, there is a right turn that would take you to Hastings Creek and the Magnolia Ranch location. Stay straight to rejoin the original trail and the return to the parking area.

Regardless of the option that you choose, you will hike about five miles and enjoy some great vistas, a pleasant stop at the river, and friendly fellow hikers. If you return here in April, the wildflowers will be putting on a great display. However, there will also be more of a crowd with the warmer weather, and the threat of a rattlesnake encounter increases significantly. This trail is not a suitable summer hike as there are many exposed sections and the temperature will be too warm for you and your pup. We make this a regular trail during the rainy season since with its exposure to the sun it dries quickly, leaving you with only a few muddy spots to traverse.

Share with: Bikers, joggers, and equestrians

> **After the hike:** Go south on Highway 49 for 1.5 miles to find **Hart to Hart Winery/Everhart Cellars** on your left. They offer wine tasting Thursday – Sunday, from 11:30 to 5:30.

3 – Lake Clementine Trail
North Fork American River
Auburn, CA

Difficulty: 2
Distance: 2.1 miles
Elevation: 365' gradual steep climb up to road, then 300' drop to the dam (return climb)

Before the hike: Stop at **Coloma Club Café** at 7171 Highway 49 (at Marshall Road) for a fine home-style breakfast. (Seasonal dog-friendly outdoor dining) (530) 626-6390

Directions: At the junction of Highway 49 and Old Foresthill Road south of Auburn (where the Highway 49 Bridge crosses the confluence of the North and Middle Forks American River), take Old Foresthill

Road about 0.25 miles and cross the Old Foresthill Bridge. Immediately after crossing the bridge, the trailhead is at the green gate on your left, marked with the number 139. Parking is available on either side of the road. Day Use Parking Fee in 2017 is $10.00 (free with an annual pass – see Resources for pass information), but there is still free parking available at No Hands Bridge Trailhead with just and additional 0.2-mile hike to the Lake Clementine Trailhead.

Description: This 2.1-mile trail takes you upstream along the North Fork American River, featuring a walk under the new Foresthill Bridge and culminating at the spillway for Lake Clementine. Along the way are marked posts 5-10 pointing out spots of interest. For detailed descriptions, and historical background, contact the Auburn State Recreation Area for their self-guided pamphlet (530-885-4527).

The trail starts out level with Marker #5 at the beginning, inviting you to gaze at the Foresthill Bridge ahead. Built originally to accommodate the lake generated by the now abandoned Auburn Dam project, the bridge is now the tallest one in California at 730 feet. Marker #6 points to the lack of larger trees in the area due to many fires in the area. At Marker #7, you see the remaining concrete abutments for the old steel bridge, which stood there from 1911-1955. Marker #8 again points to the new bridge and a closer look at its concrete abutments.

At about 0.7 miles, Marker #9 designates the beginnings of Clarks Hole, a section of still water along the river popular for swimming in the summer, and for year round fishing. A bar in the river of raised sand and boulders forms the hole. Between Marker #9 and #10 (about 0.75 miles), there is safe access down to the water and a nice beach (take care on the spur trail, as it can be slippery).

At the last post, Marker #10, you look across the river to see the remains of an old covered wooden bridge in service from 1875-1911. The bridge served to collect tolls for travelers between Foresthill and Auburn. For the less-ambitious hikers, this will be your perfect turnaround point.

Continuing beyond the last marker, the trail steadily climbs along a wide dirt service road. At about the 1-mile point, there is a spur trail to a nice fishing spot (150-foot drop from main trail to river). After another

0.25 mile, you can hear the flow from Lake Clementine ahead and peek through the trees to see the spillway waters in the distance. At 1.8 miles, you exit the trail through Gate #140 and walk to the road. Bear a sharp left into the Lake Clementine SRA through Gate #166 and continue down this road about 0.3 miles to a spur trail on your left taking you to the spillway. The entrance here is marked with a "No Dogs Allowed" sign, but you will not be entering the park, juts walking down the access road. Here you will have a great view of Lake Clementine and the North Fork Dam, the cascading water and its cool spray.

The water flows from the North Fork American River can be swift in January, so be sure to keep your dog leashed for safety along the trail. Your dog should be able to visit Clarks Hole safely, nevertheless, and there is a small waterfall for drinking water just before you reach Gate #140.

Share with: Bikers and joggers

4 – Hidden Falls Regional Park
Auburn, CA

Difficulty: 2
Distance: 6.2-mile loop
Elevation: 400' drop from trailhead to falls lookout

Directions: From I-80 in Auburn, you exit onto Highway 49 in the direction of Grass Valley. Drive west on Highway 49 for 2.7 miles and make a left turn onto Atwood Road. After 1.8 miles on Atwood, the road merges with and becomes Mt. Vernon Road. In another 0.5 miles, Mt. Vernon makes a sharp left with Joeger Road merging in from the right. Stay on Mt. Vernon here and continue another 2.1 miles to a right turn onto Mears Drive.

Follow signs for Hidden Falls Regional Park, turning onto Mears Place in 0.5 miles. Continue 0.4 miles into the park, and follow the signs to the large parking area for the park. There are plenty of car parking spaces, as well as larger spaces for horse trailers – do not park an automobile in the trailer parking spots. As spring approaches, this trail becomes overcrowded and parking spots fill. There is talk of charging a $10.00 fee to park here as well.

Description: Formerly Didion Ranch, Placer County acquired these 221 acres and developed 7.0 miles of trails down to Coon and Deadman creeks. There is an observation deck for viewing the 20' Hidden Falls and a trail with a natural overlook down to Seven Pools. Described here is a great way to visit all of the points of interest in the park. You can study the map at the parking area to review the described route.

Starting from the parking area, stay to the right of the restrooms and start on the dirt road trail called Pond Turtle Road / Trail (you will be returning on the dirt path below it). The trail takes you down 300' to a bridge crossing in 0.6 miles. After crossing the bridge, take the next trail option to the left to start on Hidden Falls Trail.

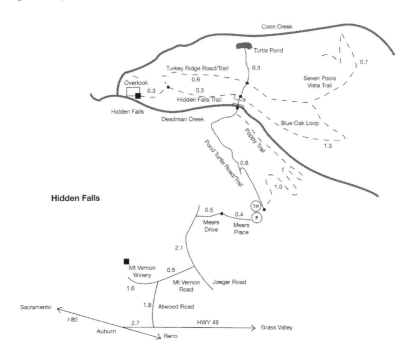

Hidden Falls Trail parallels Deadman Creek on its way to the overlook. At one point, you reach a cattle gate, so make sure you close it once you are through. The dirt path narrows, reaching an area with fence posts in 0.5 miles, and a sign below you on the left directing you to the overlook. You take this trail another 0.3 miles to the large deck from where you can see Hidden Falls. From the falls, there is a spur trail taking you lower to the creek and some nice pools of water.

When you finish your visit to the falls, return to the fence post area. From here, you continue your loop to the left, now on Turkey Ridge Road Trail. Continue on Turkey Ridge Road for 0.6 miles to its junction with Pond Turtle and Blue Oak Loop. A good choice here is to take the short 0.3-mile trip down Pond Turtle on your left and let your pooch splash in the turtle pond at the bottom.

From the pond, return to Turkey Ridge and continue your loop until you reach the junction with Blue Oak Loop and Seven Pools Vista Trail. Take the vista trail to the left for 0.7 miles to visit the seven pools along this section of Coon Creek. Return to the junction with

Turkey Ridge, and now take the Blue Oak Loop back to the bridge. Cross the bridge and take Poppy Trail 1.0 miles for the return trip to the parking area. Although you gain 300' from the bridge, there are numerous switchbacks to make it less difficult. There is a spur trail along this section taking you down to a bench at Deadman Creek and a small waterfall.

Plan a leisurely 2.5 hours of traversing the various trails and enjoying the scenery here at Hidden Falls Regional Park. Ample signage at trail junctions helps you to decide which trails you want to take to make this a pleasurable outing.

Share with: Bikers and equestrians (this is an excellent trail for beginner mountain bikes).

FEBRUARY

5. Red Shack Trail
6. Pioneer Express Trail
7. Nevada Beach
8. Snowshoeing at Loon Lake

This month, the foothill trails and snowshoeing in the mountains are the focal point. On the Pioneer Express Trail, you may encounter some early wildflowers. Nevada Beach will definitely be enjoyable, with or without snow. If the season's snowfall is low, you can still do the Loon Lake outing to Chipmunk Bluff or walk around down at the lake – the other snowshoe trails at Loon Lake need ample snow to make them doable.

Berts Lake Trail

5 – Red Shack Trail
Placerville, CA

Difficulty: 3
Distance: 1.5 miles to South Fork American River
Elevation: Downhill to the river, but steep return ascent of 850'

Directions: On Highway 49 between Coloma and Placerville, find the Red Shack produce stand and the parking area for the trail across the highway. From Coloma, you go 5.6 miles on Highway 40 toward Placerville to reach the trail. Coming into Placerville from Sacramento on Highway 50, turn left at Spring Street (second light) and go 3.5 miles on Highway 49 toward Coloma. It is a very small parking area, but sufficient for the number of visitors here.

Description: This is a 1.5 mile hike down to the South Fork American River with an elevation drop of about 850 feet, so be prepared to make an 850-foot ascent over 1.5 miles on the return trip. There are enough switchbacks on the old dirt road used for a trail to ease the climb somewhat. Still, I would rate this hike a '3' in difficulty – it is not for those with a weak heart or knees.

It takes about 30 minutes down the canyon to the river and 35 minutes back up to the trailhead. Just before reaching the bottom of the trail, you cross an old ditch once used for conducting water from Chili Bar to Lotus (Coloma-Lotus Ranch Ditch). Plan to spend time at the river to take pictures, watch kayakers, and enjoy a picnic lunch in the sun before your return trip.

After the hike, you can read the historical marker a few feet away from the parking area, to learn about the Luse Ditch Flume, and then continue on Highway 49 into Placerville and a walk on Main Street. (Cross Highway 50 at the light in Placerville, then turn left and continue straight to Main Street while Highway 49 will wind away to the right.)

We like doing this trail whenever we are short on time but still want a little exercise, often choosing to hike here before the big football game this month. This is our way to get a quick hike in for the day and still have time to watch the game. If you do not have other plans for the day, however, you are close to historic Main Street in Placerville for a nice stroll and window-shopping. It is a very dog-friendly town and well worth the visit.

6 – Pioneer Express Trail
Folsom Lake State Recreation Area
Rattlesnake Bar

Difficulty: 1-3, depending on your chosen distance
Distance: 2.1 miles to Avery's Pond
            5.5 miles to Manhattan Bar
            10.0 miles to Auburn Dam Overlook
Elevation: Mostly rolling (10'-35' undulations) with 100' gain over
      first 4.5 miles

Directions: Traveling on Auburn-Folsom Road from Folsom toward Auburn, you drive 12.4 miles to Newcastle Road (from Folsom Crossing, this is just 10.9 miles to Newcastle Road). Turn right onto Newcastle Road, and continue 1.0 miles to a "Y" intersection with Rattlesnake Road. Stay to the right at the "Y", remaining on Newcastle Road. Continue another 1.0 miles to a small parking area just before the park kiosk. This is the off-season for the park, so the vehicle gate may be closed, but the trails are still open for hiking.

For an alternate route, you could also travel on I-80 to Newcastle Road Exit and head east on Newcastle Road, crossing Auburn-Folsom Road, and then follow the directions above from the turn onto Newcastle Road.

Description: This is a scenic, relaxing stroll along the North Fork American River, on a path not heavily used, and not accessible to mountain bikers. You may see joggers and equestrians on this peaceful journey. Be sure to check your envy at the door before the drive along Auburn-Folsom Road – you are going to pass by expansive homes, equestrian paradises, and the pricey Los Lagos community.

Starting from the park entrance, walk 0.3 miles down the road and make a left to continue on the pavement. Walk another 0.1 mile to find the start of the trail marked only with a sign indicating no bikes allowed. You hike in the direction of Auburn with a very gradual uphill ascent on a rolling dirt path. Starting at the 46 mile-marker, there are additional markers every 0.5 mile. Early wildflowers are miner's lettuce, shooting stars, buttercup, and blue dick. In another month, globe lily, pretty face, lupine, wild carnation, and Indian pink will join the colorful mix. Poison oak is dormant now, but you need to keep to the trail since it can still cause a reaction even in its winter state. At this time of the year, ticks are thriving, so it is best to dress in long-sleeved and light-colored clothing for easy detection. Be sure your dog has a tick collar and monthly applications of tick repellant.

In 0.6 miles, you come to a trail marker giving you mileages. From here, it is just 1.1 miles to Avery's Pond, an appealing little bass, blue gill, and turtle pond. The trail goes in either direction around the pond, with the main trail being the one to the right. Either path merges to continue on the main Pioneer Express Trail. There are picnic tables at the pond area, as well as an easy access spot to the river for a brief sojourn.

The trail continues now along the river, and then emerges at a service road. Follow the road upstream to the Newcastle Powerhouse and a bridge taking you back to the main trail. You can hike as far as you like, stopping at the many grassy access spots to the river. There is plenty of water along the trail, so you do not need to carry any extra for your dog. We did see a coyote on this trail.

Share with: Joggers and equestrians (no bikes allowed).

7 – Nevada Beach
Zephyr Cove, NV

Difficulty: 1
Distance: 1-2 miles
Elevation: Flat

Directions: From Stateline, continue into Nevada on Highway 50 past the casinos toward Carson City. Immediately beyond the Lakeside Inn Casino, turn left at the light onto Kahle Drive. The parking area is immediately on your right.

Description: Start walking along the bike trail, making your way eventually to the shores of Lake Tahoe. There are many trail options throughout the park, some paved and some dirt paths. In February, they may be snow-covered.

Nevada Beach

You can walk toward the lake and enjoy Nevada Beach, with nice views across the water. From there, you can head into the meadows along the trails, reading some informational signs about the Indians once inhabiting the area. The trails are all flat, making for a leisurely stroll.

This is a fun place to visit in February when the snow has blanketed the meadow. Seasons are changeable, so one year there could be plenty of snow, and another may be bare. In a snowy year, you can still generally walk the trails easily enough without snowshoes since the terrain is so flat. It is a popular trail with the friendly locals walking their socialized dogs, so it gets plenty of traffic to groom the trail for easy walking. In addition to the snow play and the lake itself, you cross a small stream toward the start of the trail, and your dog can enjoy playing here as well.

This is a year round fun family excursion, except for the more restrictive summer months when the campground at Nevada Beach is in operation. You will not be able to let your dog run freely at the beach in the summer. For a good dog-friendly summer beach at Lake Tahoe, see the Kiva Beach description in the October section of this book.

8 – Snowshoe Trails at Loon Lake
Ice House Road

Various options exist at Loon Lake for a snowshoe outing, and depending on your desires for distance, you can combine them and do more than one in a single day. If snow is sparse, you can still enjoy the hike to Chipmunk Bluff.

Difficulty: 2-3 (varies with snow conditions and route chosen)

Directions: From Highway 50 going east, turn left onto Ice House Road immediately after crossing the bridge over the South Fork American River (about 22 miles east of Placerville). Follow Ice House Road for 24.3 miles to a right turn toward Loon Lake. Proceed 4.5 miles to the road into Loon Lake Campground. In February, the campground service gate is closed and you will have to park outside of the campground entrance. This is the parking for the trail to the Loon Lake Chalet and the Glissade Trail. (A service gate crosses wide paths to limit access to service and emergency vehicles only. A number of trailheads start at such a gate that you simply walk around to gain entrance. Never park in front of any gate and block its access to authorized vehicles. You could hinder emergency access and be ticketed.)

Loon Lake Chalet Trail
From the Campground Road Parking

Difficulty: 2
Distance: 1.25 miles to Chalet
Elevation: 35' gain from trailhead to Chalet

Description: The whole family will enjoy this snowshoeing trail. Here you will get to test your tracking abilities to find the trail markers along the way.

From the parking area along the road, walk 0.2 mile on the campground road to the trailhead on your left. You should see a blue diamond marker on a tree ahead of your starting point. In addition to the diamond markers, there are numerous ribbons tied to trees to mark your way. Always look ahead to the next marker before going forward. If you look backwards, you will see the diamonds on the other side of the tree for your return trip.

After 0.5 mile, the trail crosses an asphalt service road. Look ahead in your original direction, across the road, and spot your next blue diamond marker. In another 0.1 mile, you will reach a pond that may or may not be frozen. The trail diverts you around the pond, so follow the diamond markers to avoid possibly breaking through into the icy water. At 0.75 mile, you will reach a gravel service road to a power plant. The main road is immediately to your left.

Walk up to the main road and go right 0.15 mile to the Chalet. You will see the sign for the Loon Lake Chalet on your left. The Chalet provides a great picnic spot with a large deck and benches and tables (and toilet facilities). Keep your dog leashed within the Chalet area. After April 1, private parties can rent the Chalet, but you should still be able to enjoy the outdoor deck. Return on your same route – easier now as you can follow your own tracks.

If you want to continue your adventure, then snowshoe down the campground road to reach Loon Lake. The lake is beautiful this time of the year, with its frozen patches and snowy boundaries, creating silver reflections. With luck, you will visit on a sunny day, and you can make use of one of the picnic tables overlooking the lake.

Glissade Trail
From the Campground Road Parking

Difficulty: 2
Distance: 0.6-mile loop trail (plus 0.2 miles to trailhead)
Elevation: 150' climb to top of loop

Description: Enjoy a spring day of snowshoeing in El Dorado National Forest at Loon Lake. Bring a camera for shots of the distant peaks of the Crystal Range. Starting from the parking area off the road, walk down the campground road for 0.3 kilometers (0.2 miles) to the trail signpost. This is just on the opposite side of the campground road from the trail to the Loon Lake Chalet. From here, take the trail to the right, which is the Glissade Trail loop.

Do the 1.0 kilometer (0.6 miles) loop in a counterclockwise direction. You can easily see the first blue diamond just uphill from the road. This trail is very well marked, with a combination of blue diamonds in the trees and ribbons on branches. You are going to snowshoe uphill the first part of the loop, gaining about 150' in elevation.

Your climb is toward a summit, but the trail will not take you to the very top as it is too steep for a safe climb on the last part. The loop ends the uphill climb short of the top with the last diamond on a dead, broken tree stump. From here, you can look out toward the east at the Crystal Range peaks – Tells Peak is the shorter one at 8872' and McConnell Peak is the taller one at 9099'.

Now the loop heads downhill back toward the road. On the way, you see Brown Mountain (7144') directly ahead of you. When you reach the bottom of the trail back at the road, you can continue to the right in the direction of Loon Lake Campground another 0.4 kilometers (0.24 miles) for a picnic or take the trail to the Chalet to extend your outing.

Share with: Cross-country skiers (do not snowshoe over a cross-country skier's tracks).

Chipmunk Bluff
From Loon Lake Chalet

Difficulty: 3
Distance: 2.5 kilometers to bluff (1.5 miles)
Elevation: 200' gain to bluff

Directions: Heading East on Highway 50, turn left onto Ice House Road and the Crystal Basin Recreation Area immediately after crossing the bridge over the South Fork American River (about 22 miles east of Placerville). Follow Ice House Road for 24.3 miles to a right turn to Loon Lake. Proceed 5.3 miles to the entrance for Loon Lake Chalet on the left.

Description: This aerobic outing in El Dorado National Forest offers great 360-degree views as a reward. While the distance and elevation gains are not great, any snowshoeing outing requires more effort than the numbers might indicate. If the temperature exceeds 50 degrees, the snow gets slushy and even more difficult to traverse.

Starting from the back of the parking lot, locate the sign for the Chipmunk Bluff Trail that takes you to Chipmunk Bluff in 2.5 kilometers (1.5 miles). The trail is wide and is well marked with blue diamonds on trees. After hiking over the first small hill, distant mountains and peaks fill your view on the right, rewarding you for your efforts. To your left, there is a hill that you could imagine packing a snowboard up and then skiing back down.

Continuing on our trail, the views improve and the grade ascends slightly. You will be glad you have been doing your cardio at the gym in preparation. Once you come to the bluff, the diamonds end – there is no trail beyond the bluff. Depending on the snow and your abilities, you can make your way as far up the bluff as you feel safe doing, or remain below and photograph the rock formation contentedly.

Return using the same route back to the chalet and enjoy a lunch on the wood deck. Feel free to pack a feast you can leave in your car for your return (bears are hibernating for the winter).

Berts Lake Trail
From Loon Lake Chalet

Difficulty: 2+
Distance: 1.5 kilometers to lake (0.9 miles)
Elevation: 268' gain to lake

Directions: Follow directions for Chipmunk Bluff to reach the Loon Lake Chalet and the trailhead for Berts Lake Trail.

Description: After your lunch break, if you have more energy, try the Berts Lake Trail that also starts from the chalet. This is a 1.5 kilometers (0.9 miles) trail to Berts Lake, with an elevation gain of 268'.

The trail is liberally marked with diamonds and ribbons in the trees. Within fifteen minutes, you can look down at a great view of frozen Loon Lake. At one point, a metal post marks the way. Continue straight at the post to find the next diamond and to arrive at Berts Lake. If you go up the hill at this point instead, you will arrive above the lake and a great viewing area (additional 100' elevation gain). From this vantage point, you can look out to Chipmunk Bluff.

Staying straight and following all of the markers in the trees, you should successfully arrive at your destination. Expect Berts Lake to be frozen or snow-covered at this time of the year. Do not attempt to cross it or allow your dog to venture in and possibly break through the ice.

Notes: If you are new to snowshoeing, consider first one of the REI Outdoor School outings to learn about the sport. They provide the equipment, guides, and transportation for a fun group outing (fees required). They also offer a one-day Winter Trails Day event to try snowshoes and cross country equipment.

MARCH

9. Quarry Road
10. Baldwin Beach
11. Dave Moore Nature Area
12. South Yuba River State Park

If you loved snowshoeing at Loon Lake, then try Baldwin Beach this month. Otherwise, continue to enjoy the many foothill trails and their great wildflower displays.

South Fork American River at Dave Moore Nature Area

9 – Quarry Road Trail
Auburn State Recreation Area
Middle Fork American River

Difficulty: First 1.25 miles level, a '1' difficulty; remaining miles a '2' difficulty

Distance: 5.6 miles one-way (you can shorten)

Elevation: 270' overall gain, with several 50'-100' undulations

Directions: On Highway 49 between Cool and Auburn, 0.25 mile south of the American River crossing at Old Foresthill Road, you will find the parking area for Quarry Road Trail on the river's side of the highway. The trailhead is at the far end of the parking area. As with many trails in the Auburn State Recreation Area, there is currently (2017) a $10.00 parking fee (free with an annual pass).

Description: This is a scenic walk in the canyon of the Middle Fork American River. You start upstream on a wide, flat trail for the first 1.25 miles, so even those with physical limitations should be able to enjoy this part. Tricycles, strollers, and walkers will work on the first part of the trail. Two spots (at 0.2 and 0.6 mile) have picnic tables, and then at the 1.25 mark there is a large picnic area. For the less ambitious, or families with small children, plan to do this part of the walk and then return to your car. Children will have fun watching geese and ducks sunning on rocks or leisurely floating, and finding spots to scramble down to the water.

For the more adventurous hikers, continue from the picnic area, bearing right up the trail going uphill. Here, you will pass by remains of an old limestone-loading platform, a tunnel, and a cave welcoming you for a peek inside. The trail leaves the river canyon as you cross by a number of streams flowing into the river. At the 2.0-mile mark, you will intersect with the Western States Trail, where you will continue in the direction of Brown's Bar Trail, with the trail returning closer to the river.

Soon you will begin to hear the sounds coming from the off-road vehicles at the Mammoth Bar Off-Highway Vehicle (OHV) Park across the river. You can pause on your side of the river and watch the bikes traversing the dirt paths up the canyon walls. The sound will carry with you along the trail for a while, but it is dim enough so as not to be an annoyance.

Foothill brush, oaks, madrones, olive trees, buckeyes, and digger pines line the trail. Beware the blackberry vines and poison oak plants along the sides. It is a well-maintained trail, so as long as you avoid going off-trail, you should not have any problems.

At 2.75 miles, the trail descends close to the river's edge, making for easy access to its bank. This is a nice resting place (and possible turnaround). Continuing on, at 3.5 miles, you reach the Brown's Bar Trail. Stay on the Western States Trail in the direction of Maine Bar Trail. At 4.5 miles, again the trail touches down to river level. Although you will have to cross a field of river rocks to reach its edge, you have easy access to a nice deep, clear, pool of calm water. This is again a possible turnaround point or you can continue on the trail, now narrower, another mile to the intersection with the Maine Bar Trail, before ending at Maine Bar at 5.6 miles.

The scenery is beautiful on this very popular trail. You will encounter bikers, joggers, horseback riders, and families throughout your day. It is best to come earlier in the day to avoid the larger crowds.

Notes: Mammoth Bar OHV Park, part of the Auburn State Recreation Area, has no fees and is open year round (canyon trails closed on Saturdays). It features 1200 acres, combining scenic steep canyon and river rides on well-marked and maintained trails. A beginner's loop is available as well.

10 – Baldwin Beach
South Lake Tahoe
Snowshoeing

Difficulty: 1

Distance: Varies on route choice, but you could go 2.5 miles on the snow-covered bike trail

Elevation: Flat route at about 6300'

Directions: At the "Y" in South Lake Tahoe, where Highway 50 veers to the right toward the casinos, stay straight and onto Highway 89 in the direction of Tahoe City. Drive 4.0 miles to Camp Richardson, just past marker 48, and park along the roadway at the entrance for Baldwin Beach (now closed for the winter). If parking is full, you can park anywhere along the roadway starting at marker 46 and pick up the bike trail, most likely snow-covered. Never park in such a way as to block an entrance gate.

Description: When Baldwin Beach is open for the season, dogs are not allowed on the beach. In the winter, while the beach is closed, dogs are allowed (there is a leash ordinance). This is a great opportunity to enjoy the area with your pooch and be legal. We discovered this beach one winter when we found Highway 89 closed beyond this point due to snow and driving conditions. If you are ever on your way to other trails beyond here (such as Eagle Falls or Meeks Creek) and find the highway closed, remember that you can still enjoy a day at Baldwin Beach.

From the entrance gate, you can walk toward the lake to enjoy the beach. There are picnic tables and benches throughout the area (bathroom facilities will be closed for the season). You have a great view of Mt. Tallac from the beach, and you can enjoy the serenity of Lake Tahoe in winter. Taylor Creek will block you from walking beyond Baldwin Beach to Kiva Beach.

The other option here is to start from the parking area and head to your right along the bike trail. With this route, you have a bridge crossing Taylor Creek and you can continue 2.5 miles on this route, taking in Tallac Historic Site along the way. At Tallac, you can view refurbished estates and outbuildings from the 1920's. At the far end of the route, you have a view out to Tahoe Keys. You do not have to stay on the bike trail, as there are many opportunities to walk toward Lake Tahoe and enjoy its beaches.

This is a great opportunity to enjoy the serenity of winter at one of summer's popular beaches. If walking around Baldwin Beach is too tame for you, try across the highway on trails around Fallen Leaf Lake for longer routes and more opportunity to explore.

11 – Dave Moore Nature Area
South Fork American River
Lotus, CA

Difficulty: 1
Distance: 1.0-mile loop trail (including spur trails)
Elevation: 80' change in elevation

Before the hike: Stop at **Sierra Rizing Bakery** to pick up some treats or maybe a bread loaf for tonight's dinner. The bakery is immediately across the bridge on the left in Lotus. (530) 642-1308

Directions: From Highway 50 in Shingle Springs, take the Ponderosa Road exit #37 and go north across the freeway. After crossing the freeway, turn right onto North Shingle Road at the light immediately after the signal for the westbound off-ramp (signed Lotus, Coloma, Georgetown, Rescue, No. Shingle Rd.). North Shingle Road merges with and becomes Green Valley Road after 4.0 miles. In 0.4 miles, Green Valley Road veers to the right. Stay straight here and you will now be on Lotus Road. In 6.8 miles, Lotus Road will dead end at Highway 49.

When Lotus Road dead ends at Highway 49, turn left and cross the bridge over the South Fork American River. In 1.0 mile after crossing the bridge, you will see the rock wall entrance for the Dave Moore Nature Area on your left. (If the entrance gate is closed, park outside the park and walk down to the trailhead.)

Coming from the other direction, from I-80 in Auburn, connect with Highway 49 south toward Cool. The entrance to the nature area will be on your right about 3.0 miles south of Pilot Hill. From Placerville, take Highway 49 through Coloma. At the three-way stop at Lotus Road and Highway 49, continue straight across the bridge. Go 1.0 mile after the bridge to find the entrance on the left.

Description: This is an easy hike, maintained by the Bureau of Land Management (BLM). The trail features many picnic tables and access to the American River. Most importantly, the first part of the hike is accessible to anyone physically challenged. A monument with a plaque is located at the start of your walk honoring Dave Moore, a BLM employee afflicted with multiple sclerosis at the age of 35. His co-workers and other volunteers worked together to create a nature area that all could enjoy. (The trail often needs maintenance after a storm to return it to a suitable condition for the physically challenged.)

Start the hike from the parking area in a counter-clockwise direction. After passing numerous streams and some picnic tables (two specifically designed for wheelchair access), you will come to an interesting rock at 0.2 mile. The rock's composition is such that its center eroded more quickly (from wind and other elements), forming a mushroom-like appearance.

The trail then turns into an area with large ponderosa pines with their "patchwork" bark, their needles blanketing your walk. At 0.26 mile, you will come to a grand madrone tree with its beautiful reddish bark. Round the bend to find a rock wall lining the way and listen for the river ahead. It is just a few minutes now to the spur trail taking you down to the South Fork American River.

Pause here at the river and enjoy its peacefulness. In the coming months, there will be a constant stream of rafts and kayakers maneuvering their way down the river's rocky lanes. Another beach awaits you, so return to the main trail to continue the loop. (For the physically challenged, this is the turnaround spot, since the trail will now narrow and is uneven and rocky for a while.)

In less than 0.1 mile, you will see a large boulder bordering the left side of the trail. Just before the rock, a spur trail takes off to your right, returning you to the river and a nice beach with beautiful black sand beckoning you to gold panning. If this beach is occupied, continue along the beach upstream to an equally nice alternative.

Leaving the river, the trail again becomes even and easy to navigate. It is dotted with beautiful rock formations. Some spurs exist, but stay on the main trail (the BLM have marked off the spurs with branches and burlap rolls to indicate they are closed). Start a short ascent now, with the trail lined with manzanita shrubs. After the climb, you will head back through a grove of oaks, cross a bridge, and return to the parking area. Just across the bridge (before the parking area), there is a picnic area up the hill.

For the physically challenged having to turn around at the river and not complete the loop, cross the bridge at the other end of the loop and go 200 feet in a clockwise direction. This will take you to a wonderful spot for wildflowers, with baby blue-eyes, five spots (early bloomers), and many more to enjoy and photograph. You can continue in this direction for a while before needing to turn around again.

You can return to the nature area in the coming weeks to find a constant display of new wildflowers emerging weekly, such as pretty face, California poppies, globe lilies, and lacepod. On your revisit, do the loop in the reverse direction and you will definitely see new parts and angles of the trail to photograph or sketch. Return throughout the year to experience the different seasons and enjoy the river at different water levels. Things change constantly here, and every time you visit, you are sure to see something new.

12 – South Yuba River State Park
Bridgeport, CA

There are two trail choices at South Yuba River State Park, and both well worth the trip. If we are planning to do the popular Buttermilk Bend Trail, we usually first do Pt. Defiance to burn some of our dog's energy before the more controlled, leashed walk to view the wildflowers.

The decision for the best month to visit here was difficult – too early and the wildflowers are not in bloom, but too late and the poison oak is difficult to avoid on the narrow stretches of the trail. March is a good choice, therefore, for the Pt. Defiance trail, and you will appreciate cool weather for the initial climb and the wildflowers at Buttermilk Bend. Be careful, nevertheless, to avoid the poison oak beginning to leaf out.

Directions: In Grass Valley, from Highway 49, take the exit for Highway 20 to Marysville and Penn Valley. Go 7.8 miles on Highway 20 into Penn Valley and turn right onto Pleasant Valley Road. Travel 7.8 miles to the South Yuba River State Park. Drive past the parking near the visitor center and cross the bridge to find another parking area on your right. Originally, the parking was at the visitor center for the Pt. Defiance Trail, but the covered bridge is closed for repair and the river crossing is not currently accessible. Now the further parking area serves for both trail options.

Warning: Respect the park's rules about dogs not allowed on the beach areas along the river in the immediate park area. Also, note limited access May-September for dogs. There is a $5.00 parking fee at the park.

Pt. Defiance Trail to Englebright Lake

Difficulty: 2
Distance: 2.8-mile loop
Elevation: 380' climb

Description: This is a fun hike, especially for your dog, with lots of opportunities to run down to the river for a splash. For the naturalist, you walk through a variety of habitats, starting with foothill chaparral and oaks, then canyon buckeyes and madrones, and then the riparian river habitat of willows and cottonwoods. For the historian, the park features one of only ten covered bridges remaining in California.

The trail originally started by walking across the covered bridge, but the bridge is currently closed, waiting for funds and approvals for historical repairs. Wood's Bridge is the longest existing covered bridge in the United States. Built in 1862, it spans 251 feet across the South Fork Yuba River. With the bridge closed, you need to start the trail upstream. From the parking area, carefully cross the roadway to the service road and immediately find the trailhead pointing 1.7 miles to Pt. Defiance to your right.

This first part of the trail consists of switchbacks taking you up a 380-foot hill lush with native brush and oaks. At the top, there is a picnic table for a short break. Continuing on the trail, you walk through a meadow, cross a bridge, and then arrive at a service gate. Walk around (or under) the gate and continue down the service road, getting views of Englebright Lake and the Yuba River Canyon on your right. This is a steep descent and can be slippery if wet, so take care on the way down. Later in the spring, you can enjoy the array of blue-purple wildflowers, such as blue dick, bush lupine, bowel-tube iris, and larkspur along this portion of the trail. There is also a small grouping of California Indian pink along the service road descent. In this same area, you can also find both the California Pipe Vine and Manroot (wild cucumber vine). You bottom out at the confluence of the river and the lake, and a small picnic area shaded by willows. Here you can sit and watch any boaters as you take a break.

Continuing the loop, the trail narrows as it parallels the river. This 1-mile section is difficult in sections, with rocks to climb over and around, and steep drop-offs. You can reach the river to try some gold panning at a number of spur trails (early spurs are quite steep, but as you near the bridge area you will find a couple easier routes). The last part of the trail offers you splendid views of the covered bridge. Take time to look into the Visitor Center (open Thursday – Sunday from 11:00 am to 5:00 pm) and enjoy the rest of the park and its history before returning home. Return here in October for the "Fall Festival" at the park. Check southyubariverstatepark.org or phone (530) 432-1261 for the date.

Buttermilk Bend

Difficulty: 1
Distance: 1.2 miles (one-way)
Elevation: 75' gain – mostly flat trail

Description: The Buttermilk Bend trail starts at the left end of the parking area. The trail parallels the South Fork Yuba River for its 1.2-mile length. The first half should be suitable for those with walkers. You should plan on leashing and scooping for your dog on this very popular trail. At the peak of wildflower season, it can be crowded.

Along the way, you will find numerous wildflowers and native brush with labeled markers for easy identification. There are many picture-taking opportunities of the flowers and the beautiful river below. Be on the lookout for flowers without labels, such as a display of petite red maids at the start of the trail. Labeled flowers include globe lily, caterpillar phacelia, foothill penstemon, rosy clover, larkspur, Chinese houses, and multiple varieties of poppies and lupine.

In addition, numerous spur trails offer a path down to the river for a break and a splash for your dog. The trail itself has a number of benches for stops and a bridge crossing a nice creek with access to it above the bridge. If you use a walker, then the bridge will be your turn around point.

This trail could easily accommodate those with physical limitations, so everyone in the family can enjoy this outing. At times, there are steep drop-offs, so if you are afraid of precipices you may want to reconsider taking this hike.

April

13. Bassi Falls
14. Darrington Bike Trail
15. Fairy Falls
16. Feather Falls

This month features a number of great waterfalls to visit as well as a bike trail with wildflowers and access to Folsom Lake. The new route to Bassi Falls takes you on a trail with abundant spots to access Big Silver Creek and the outlet stream from Bassi Falls. The drive to Fairy Falls may seem too long, but the wildflowers and the waterfall itself make up for the miles.

Lower Bassi Falls

13 – Bassi Falls
Crystal Basin Recreation Area

Difficulty: 2

Distance: 2 miles to falls from trailhead (add 0.6 miles if parked at Ice House Road)

Elevation: 400' gain

Directions: From Highway 50 East, about 5.0 miles past Fresh Pond, take the left turn onto Ice House Road toward the Crystal Basin Recreation Area. Drive 16.4 miles just across the bridge for Big Silver Creek and opposite the Big Silver Creek Campground. If the Road 12N32A is posted, "Closed to Vehicles", then park off Ice House Road and walk in to the trailhead (the Forest Service closes vehicle access seasonally and reopens at varying times in the spring). You are subject to ticketing if you ignore the posting.

Now either walk or continue driving in to the trailhead for 0.4 miles, staying on Road 12N32A and bypassing the alternate route signed for Bassi Falls at 0.2 miles (the service gate at this other route to the falls may or may not be closed). At the 0.4-mile mark, there is a large parking area and a road to your right taking you to the trailhead itself. You may wish to park here and walk the additional 0.2 miles down to the trailhead to avoid the rutted road.

Description: This is most likely a snowshoe outing in April, so carry your snowshoes with you, but plan on taking them off in sections and carrying them over the exposed granite. The falls are beautiful in the spring with any surrounding snow intensifying the majesty of the scene. You will find plenty to photograph here and find the effort in any snow well worth it.

From the trailhead sign, follow the path marked liberally with hiker signs in the trees. You are instantly walking along Big Silver Creek and might want to make a brief stop at the water for your dog to cool off. The trail then starts to climb briefly, gaining 150' over the first 0.7 miles as you arrive at a trail post. The post directs you forward 1.3 miles to the falls. A left here takes you to a secondary parking area at Towering Rocks. Continue in the direction of the falls.

About 30 minutes into your hike, you will gain a view of the lower falls. In another 15 minutes, you will have access to a great swimming area for your dog. From here, you will climb another 100' feet as you make your way to the falls. The path varies in terrain, sometimes taking you a forested area, then across streams, and finally a climb over large granite rocks. You will have an early glimpse of the falls on the last section of trail. Pay careful attention to your route and look for the hiker signs to make this trek successful.

At the falls, you will likely encounter few other hikers this time of the year as compared to the summer crowds. You can enjoy the lower pools and interesting rock formations. The falls themselves should be particularly impressive in the spring.

If you return here in the summer, you can take a trail to the top of the falls. While looking at the falls, find a spur trail on the left of the water. This trail will take you up to the headwaters. The first part of this trail is dirt, and then you have to make your way carefully up rocks. You are a good distance from the water, so there is no fear of falling into the falls. You do need to be careful on the rocks, however, as it would be easy to slip and fall a great distance. When you reach the top, your reward is some great views back down to the base. You will also find a nice swimming hole here.

DO NOT ATTEMPT TO WALK DIRECTLY UP THE WATERFALL ITSELF – USE THE SPUR TRAIL.

14 – Darrington Mountain Bike Trail
El Dorado Hills, CA

Difficulty: 2

Distance: Varies

Elevation: About 40' gain from trailhead with mostly a flat trail involving occasional 20' "ups and downs"

Directions: When El Dorado Hills Boulevard crosses Green Valley Road, it becomes Salmon Falls Road. Go 5.7 miles on Salmon Falls Road in the direction of Pilot Hill. You park in the gravel area on your left, just before reaching the Salmon Falls Bridge. Walk 0.16 mile across the bridge and past Skunk Hollow to the trailhead parking on your left.

Both the trailhead parking and the Skunk Hollow parking are fee, self-registration parking areas, so parking on the other side of the bridge saves you money. If you have acquired an annual California State Parks pass, then you can park free in these other areas.

Description: Bring a picnic blanket for this beautiful, easy hike. At a little short of 3.0 miles, there is a lovely open area to sit, looking out to Folsom Lake. Along the way, you cross several streams and plenty of access spots to the water for your dog. You may want to limit water access for your dog to the streams rather the lake, however, as there are patches of weeds with prickly stickers between the trail and the lake. Wildflowers are starting to come out now for your enjoyment. There is the usual potpourri of flowers such as pretty face, Applegate's paintbrush, and a variety of poppy species, but the bonus here is the great display of sunflowers along the trailside. There is no real destination, just walk for as long as you want and then turn around for the hike back to your car.

The trail starts with a short 20-foot climb before leveling out. When you reach the "Y", either choice will bring you to the same place in a short distance. The narrow, rocky, dirt trail parallels the South Fork American River. Then you will drop down to a small stream where the trail widens for awhile, taking you by fields of lupine.

Within 45 minutes, you will be at another stream crossing. Your trail is lined first with oaks and then with native brush. At 2.5 miles, there is another "Y" and again either route takes you to the same place (the left arm looks much easier). If you go beyond 3.0 miles, your elevation will rise a little.

The entire length of the trail is over 7.0 miles, so plan to hike whatever portion is comfortable and fits your time schedule. Its other end is at Peninsula Campground (often closed for the season so hard to plan parking a second vehicle here).

Share with: Bikers

15 – Fairy Falls
Spenceville Wildlife Area

Difficulty: 2
Distance: 2.5 miles to the falls
Elevation: 300' gain to falls on undulating trail

Directions: From I-80 in Auburn exit onto Highway 49 in the direction of Grass Valley. Once in Grass Valley, take the exit for Highway 20 West in the direction of Marysville. Drive 12.5 miles through Penn Valley, and turn left onto Smartville Road (signed for Beale Air Force Base). Travel 1.0 miles on Smartville Road before coming to a fork in the road. Stay left at the fork to continue on Smartville Road another 3.8 miles where you turn left onto Waldo Road. Travel 1.8 miles before coming to Waldo Bridge, built in 1901 (there is a weight limit for the bridge of 14 tons). Cross the bridge, and continue another 2.3 miles to find a large parking area for the trailhead on your left. The last part of the drive is on a gravel road.

From Marysville, you drive East on Highway 20 19.2 miles and turn right onto Smartville Road in the direction of Beale Air Force Base. Then follow the above directions starting at Smartville Road.

Description: The Spenceville Wildlife Area covers over 11,000 acres, with portions in both Yuba and Nevada Counties. The Department of Fish and Game governs the site, open for hunting during turkey and deer seasons. Call (530) 538-2236 before visiting the area to assure there are no closures during your planned visit. Visit **www.dfg.ca.gov/lands/ wa/region2/Spenceville.html** to learn more about the area. The Friends of Spenceville also have an informative site at **www.spenceville.org**.

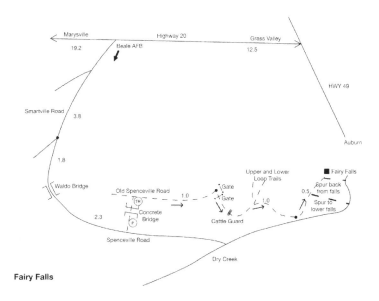

Fairy Falls

From the parking area, walk across the old concrete bridge and then turn right onto the wide dirt trail, formerly Old Spenceville Road. Continue about 1.0 miles in this direction, climbing just 200', and arrive at a gate marked with a "Falls" sign pointing you to the right. Turn right here and locate a second gate across the trail. Open the pedestrian portion of the gate (and close behind you) to continue on the trail uphill.

At the top of the 50' climb uphill, you arrive at a cattle guard and great views of the region. The wide trail continues beyond the cattle guard, winding its way down the hill to the right. (You could take the spur trail here downhill to reach the same spot.) As the main and the spur trails reunite, you find two more spur trails leading you uphill – these are the Upper and Lower Loop Trails (open to hikers only). Continue straight here on the wider old road, now named Fairy Falls Trail, for the easiest path to the falls. The other loop trails are also options for reaching the falls on less popular paths.

Your trail now takes you along hillsides resplendent in an array of wildflowers, including lupine, poppies, wild daisies, and gold nuggets (mariposa lilies). Eventually dropping 175', at the two-mile point on the wide Fairy Falls Trail, you come to an easy access spot to Dry Creek. There is a small pool here, and a nice rock formation. Over the next 0.5 miles, you have other access spots for enjoying the creek before the trail narrows for its final uphill climb of about 200' to Fairy Falls (also known as Dry Creek Falls, Beale Falls, and Shingle Falls).

The trail ends at the top of the 47' falls, but you can take a little spur trail lower for a good picture-taking spot. From this lower spot, you can see a spur trail that takes you back to the main Fairy Falls Trail. On your return hike, take a spur trail to the left taking you down to the creek and views of Lower Fairy Falls.

Bring your wildflower and bird books along with you for this trail. We spotted woodpeckers, blue jays, California bluebirds, red-winged blackbirds, cowbirds, and a red-shouldered hawk. On our return portion of the hike, we came across an alligator lizard and a ribbon snake on the trail (both harmless).

Share with: Bikers and equestrians (note some trails within the area restrict usage, but the described route is open to both).

16 – Feather Falls Trail
Feather River

Difficulty: 3
Distance: 9.5-mile loop trail
Elevation: 870' descent followed by ascents of 480' and 619'

Directions: From Highway 70 in Oroville, travel 1.8 miles east on Oroville Dam Road. Turn right onto Highway 162, the Olive Highway, and continue another 6.5 miles. Turn right onto Forbestown Road and continue 6.7 miles. Go left onto Lumpkin Road for another 11.0 miles, crossing over Lake Oroville on the Enterprise Bridge, passing a bald eagle nest, and arriving in Feather Falls. There is a sign directing you to the left for Feather Falls Trail. From here, it is just 1.6 miles to the ample parking area for the trailhead.

Alternate Route: If you are starting closer to Auburn, or you just enjoy the "back" way when driving, then consider starting from Nevada City. In Nevada City on the joined Highways 20 and 49, turn left onto Highway 49 in the direction of Downieville. Travel a total of 16.7 miles on Highway 49, passing Independence Trail, crossing the South Yuba River, and making a left onto Moonshine Road. After 4.9 miles, passing by New Bullards Bar Reservoir, turn left onto Marysville Road. In 4.3 miles, look for your right turn onto Oregon Hill Road. The road starts out with graded pavement, looking like the wrong road, but you are going in the right direction.

You drive 11.7 miles on Oregon Hill Road before arriving in the town of Challenge. Here turn left onto La Porte Road for a short 1.6-mile ride through town. Turn right onto the Challenge Cutoff for 2.6 miles, as it turns into Forbestown Road, and takes you into the small town of Forbestown. You are on Forbestown Road for 11.6 miles, and then turn right onto Lumpkin Road. You drive 11.0 miles on Lumpkin Road before coming to the signed left turn for the Feather Falls Trail. This is a fun drive, but adds an extra thirty minutes to the trip.

Description: This is a long drive and a long hike, so pack plenty of water bottles in a cooler in the car for the drive. Carry at least three bottles each for the trail, and leave a spare in the cooler for the trip home – and do not forget water for your pooch. (The parking area is very busy, so there is no need to worry about bears wanting to get into your cooler.) The reward for this effort is the fantastic view of 640' Feather Falls. Be sure to bring your camera, since the trail will guide you to a large overlook area with a direct view of the photogenic falls. Allow yourself four to five hours on the trail.

This well-maintained trail is wide enough to enable you to avoid the ample poison oak lining it. There is plenty of shade on the trail, but it can be muggy if it is a warm day. Stay on the trail and avoid the shortcuts hikers have made over the years. Also, be sure to pack out your trash to avoid adding to the deplorable waste you will likely encounter. If you have a plastic bag with you, you can do your share to pick up the litter you find along the way.

After 0.3 miles, the trail forks into the Upper and Lower Trails. Take the left fork for the Lower Trail to the falls, and you will return on the Upper Trail. The Upper Trail is 1.0 mile longer, so it makes the return ascent less strenuous. Continuing now on the Lower Trail, you arrive shortly at a rest stop shaded by a large oak. Here you can read about the large grinding stones used by the Maidu Indians and see one of the mortar holes used for grinding acorns. Frequently along the trail, you benefit from a number of similar signs explaining the view, plants, or historical significance of the spot.

The trail continues a slow descent to the first crossing of Frey Creek. Along the trail, you can enjoy the typical array of foothill wildflowers, including the largest display of Indian pink that I have ever come across. The ponderosa pines, madrones, and cedars shade your route, along with an occasional dogwood in bloom. After crossing the creek, the trail parallels it for a while, allowing you to enjoy the riparian vegetation of alders and ferns.

At 1.5 miles, you come to an opening with a great view of 3509' Bald Rock Dome across the Bald Rock Canyon rising 2000' above the Middle Fork Feather River. An informational plaque explains the regard of the dome for meditation to the Maidu and other Native Californians over many years.

At 2.25 miles, you again cross the creek, and reach the lowest point of the hike. You now have a 1.25-mile ascent of 325' before reaching the next trail junction. Here the trail marker indicates you have just 0.5 miles to the overlook. The other direction takes you on the 4.5-mile return trip on the Upper Trail.

On the 0.5-mile ascent to the overlook area, you gain another 155'. Take your time making the climb, stopping at the first rest area. At this spot, you can look down at the confluence of Fall River and the Middle Fork Feather River as they join to flow into Lake Oroville. In a year of good water storage, boaters can make it up this arm of the lake to get a close up view of the falls.

Continuing to the overlook, you come to a marker pointing to the overlook to the left. Here you can see another trail taking off uphill to the right. After your stay at the overlook, you should return to this trail for a walk over to the falls' headwaters. The overlook area gives you a picturesque view of 640' Feather Falls. It is a large decked open area with plenty of picture-taking opportunities. Feather Falls is the sixth highest in the United States and the fourth highest in California. When you are ready to leave the overlook, return to the trail, and head uphill for a trip to the headwaters.

The route to the top of the falls is an easy, short walk on a narrow trail. When you reach the top, take the first spur on your left to make your way down to the headwaters. Exercise caution in this area and keep your dog leashed for safety. You can return to the main headwaters trail and follow it a little longer away from the falls. From this trail, numerous spurs take you down to Fall River. Along this stretch, you can find areas to stop for your picnic, a nice rest, and a splash of water on your face.

For the return hike, take the Upper Trail 4.5 miles to the parking area. Along this trail, you climb constantly, with occasional dips down to Frey Creek. The first 2.5 miles climb 345'. You then descend 175' down to Frey Creek and a great viewing spot of the creek's falls. The final 1.5-mile hike climbs back 450' to the trailhead, so take time and look for the nice display of bleeding hearts lining the trail. You will definitely be tired by the time your reach your car, but I am certain you will agree the effort was well worth it.

MAY

Some of the higher mountain trails will open in May, but you should always check first to make sure of conditions. Both the Van Sickle State Park and the Caples Creek trails have service gates closed until the start of the season. These higher trails offer cooler temperatures and relief from the more crowded foothill trails, now laden with poison oak and rattlesnakes. Best to go up to the higher elevation trails whenever possible. There may still be snow patches on these trails, but they should be easily traversable.

Cinder Cone on Tahoe Rim Trail

17 – Meeks Creek Trails
Meeks Bay, CA

At Meeks Creek trailhead, you have two options for a day hike, depending on the distance you want to cover. For the easier option, stay on the Meeks Creek Trail and try a nice 4-mile loop. For a much longer outing, turn midway on the Meeks Creek Trail onto the Tahoe-Yosemite Trail and a journey into Desolation Wilderness.

Before the hike: If you forgot to pack an essential trail item, stop at Lake of the Sky Outfitters for supplies. They are next to Subway at the "Y", 1023 Emerald Bay Rd., (530) 541-1027.

Meeks Creek Trail

Difficulty: 1
Distance: 4-mile loop (or 2 miles each direction if crossing Meeks Creek is impossible)
Elevation: Flat trail, 200' gain

Directions: At the "Y" in South Lake Tahoe, leave Highway 50 as it turns to the right (becoming Lake Tahoe Blvd.), and stay straight on Highway 89 toward Tahoe City. Go 16.2 miles on Highway 89 to Meeks Bay and find the parking area on your left.

There is a Forest Service board at the trailhead with information and trail permits for Desolation Wilderness (not necessary for this hike). From the parking area, locate the green forest gate that leads you onto Forest Road 14N32 for the start of the trail.

Description: The hike is through a meadow, surrounded by hills on three sides, and Highway 89 on the fourth end. The creek is on the south end of the meadow. Other popular spots exist along Highway 89 before reaching Meeks Bay, so this is a less crowded location. You may only encounter a few other people at this spot, so you are better able to enjoy the sights and nature's sounds. Many locals use this trail to exercise their dogs, so look forward to a lot of interaction on the trail for your pup.

Your experience will vary depending on whether you can cross Meeks Creek mid-way in the hike. If there is too much water for a safe crossing, then you will have to turn around here. Consider returning in the fall to do the entire loop described. You can also come here earlier in the year to make this a snowshoe outing. It is a great, flat trail for enjoying the snow and perhaps the creek will have enough snow covering it to make it crossable.

Variable conditions on Meeks Creek Trail

The trail starts along the service road, continuing straight at first and then veering left when you approach a hill at the west end of the meadow. Continue on the path following alongside this hill. You are now heading south in the direction of the creek. At 1.4 miles, there will be a marked trail to the right leading into Desolation Wilderness. Stay straight here to continue along the road.

You will pass by a spur trail that takes you to the remains of an old camp. The stone foundation remains, along with discarded items like doors and bed frames, and you can imagine what living there would have been like. Climb up the remaining stairs and share the views of the past inhabitants before returning to the main trail.

The trail narrows for the next 0.5 miles on your route to the creek and an enjoyable lunch spot. From here, you need to determine if you can safely cross the creek, or possibly change into water shoes for the chilly experience. If not ready to take the plunge, then this is your turnaround point. If you do proceed forward, you will discover some beautiful forest scenery, spring wildflowers, and a great meadow for your dog to run. Leaving the meadow, the trail is less wooded and picturesque as you follow back in the direction of Highway 89. You emerge onto the highway just south of where you parked, but it is an easy walk back to the trailhead. The last part of the loop is less desirable, so we often make the meadow our lunch spot and turnaround to return on the original route. By making it to the meadow, you add a little distance to the trek, making for a better day hike experience.

Meeks Creek is a true year-round trail, and I return here to enjoy it in every season. It was particularly good for our old dog, Toots, as she aged and could not make the longer or more strenuous treks. In her last year, we would just hike as far as the pond for a rest and snacks before returning to our vehicle. Its easy terrain, natural beauty, and sharing with just the locals, makes for a most pleasurable day trip.

Meeks Creek
Tahoe-Yosemite Trail
Desolation Wilderness

Difficulty: 3

Distance: 4.6 miles to Lake Genevieve

4.9 miles to Crag Lake

5.6 miles to Hidden Lake

Elevation: 1,320' gain

Directions: Follow the same directions as to the parking for Meeks Creek. There is a Forest Service board at the trailhead with information and trail permits for Desolation Wilderness (free). You must fill out a Day Pass here and deposit the stub in the box. From the parking area, locate the green forest gate that leads you onto Forest Road 14N42 for the start of the trail.

Description: This trail in El Dorado National Forest starts the northern end of the Tahoe-Yosemite Trail. It is very easy to follow, with no rock slabs to cross searching for "ducks". The first part of the trail is flat, along the sandy service road (possible snow patches). After 1.4 miles along the road, you find the signage for the actual trail on your right and a pond on your left.

As soon as you start on the trail portion, you begin a climb and gain elevation. Over the next three miles, you gain 1,200'. In addition to the steepness, at times there are rock steps to contend with as well. Your first plateau is after 0.4 miles. From here, you can look back to a view of Lake Tahoe in the distance.

After the brief plateau, you again climb steeply, with dust and little shade, before finally reaching a nice flat section and your first glimpse of Meeks Creek. The area seems enchanted, with creek noises, birds calling, shade, a cool path, and an impressive array of colors lining the trail from wildflowers, ferns, and edible thimbleberries (berries taste like a raspberry and resemble a sewing thimble). Willow bushes and small alders populate this garden-like flat. The next section of the trail, often with the creek accessible, is a pleasant respite from your climb. Following this pleasant rest, you do more climbing, but it is broken up with another enjoyable flat section with meadows on your left.

At 3.2 miles along the trail, and after another 300' climb, you reach a bridge crossing over Meeks Creek. From here, you climb over rock and branch steps, gaining another 400' before finally emerging at Lake Genevieve and a trail junction. To the right, you could take the Lake Genevieve Trail over to the Pacific Crest Trail (PCT). To the left, you stay on the Meeks Bay Trail portion of the Tahoe-Yosemite Trail and continue to the next lake. Lake Genevieve itself is small, shallow, and with little beach access other than where the trail emerges. It is worth but a short rest before you continue on to Crag Lake.

It takes only minutes from the end of Lake Genevieve to climb up the 80' over 0.25 miles before reaching the more impressive Crag Lake. In the distance, you can see Crag Peak looming at 9,054'. There is a lot more beach access here at Crag Lake, as well as picturesque spots for photos. The water is deeper and better for swimming, and you can try fishing for brown trout.

The trail goes along the eastern shore of Crag Lake, then you leave the lake for another rock-hop creek crossing, a 50' climb, and 0.4 miles to another trail junction (unsigned). From this point, you can see small Hidden Lake below on your right, and the steep spur trail taking you down to its shore. You drop 50' over 0.25 miles to reach the bottom at the lake's eastern shore. Across the lake, you have an even better view of Crag Peak. This is a rock climber's access point to the peak's base and a 400' climb to its top. With luck, you can sit back, enjoy your lunch, and let some climbers entertain you.

Tahoe-Yosemite Trail: The Meeks Bay trailhead is the northern end of this 185-mile trail to Tuolumne Meadows in Yosemite. A good portion of the trail shares the route with the Pacific Crest Trail. A good time of year to attempt the entire route is July to August, figuring at least two weeks to make the journey.

Pacific Crest Trail: The PCT runs from the Mexican to the Canadian border, covering 2,650 miles. The trail travels through the Mojave Desert, the Sierras, Yosemite, and the Cascades. Annually, hundreds of hikers complete the entire journey, but thousands do portions of it each year. Visit **www.pcta.org** for more information.

18 – Van Sickle
Joint Nevada and California State Park

Difficulty:	2+ to waterfall
	3+ to Tahoe Rim Trail (TRT)
Distance:	1.1 miles to waterfall
	3.3 miles to TRT
Elevation:	544' to waterfall
	1200' to TRT

Directions: Heading east on Highway 50, you turn right onto Heavenly Village Way. This is the light just prior to reaching the state line. When Heavenly Village Way ends at Montreal, continue straight into Van Sickle State Park. Drive past the Park Host and continue .04 miles in the direction of the Equestrian Trailhead. Leave the larger parking spots for equestrians if possible.

Description: The Van Sickle State Park is a joint venture with California and Nevada. The park is open to vehicles from May to October each year. From the parking area, locate the dirt path that takes you across the road and to a kiosk with a map of the area (an earlier kiosk at the toilet area does not have an adequate map). The trail starts just beyond the kiosk.

The trail is mostly decomposed granite, making for a somewhat dusty and slippery trek. Breaking up the dirt path are occasional rock steps to ascend. The trail is exposed to the sun, and the wind can be gusty. The destination waterfall is a little underwhelming, even early in the season, and it is difficult to photograph due to its cover of vegetation. Carry water for your pooch since other than the waterfall there is no other water along the trail.

What makes this a great hike, then? It is the views you gain of the entire Lake Tahoe area, with the beaches, the colorful water with its emerald green turning to deep blue, the nearby casinos, and the distant peaks of the Sierras, primarily the handsome Mt. Tallac. With a good snow year, the peak should be sporting patches of snow at its top early in May.

After 0.4 miles, and an elevation gain of 158', there is a spur trail marked "Vista" to the right. I suggest saving this side trip for your return, as there still is a great amount of climbing to do over the next 0.7 miles. Just past the spur, you will come to a trail junction and an informational sign giving the history of the Gondola Fire. As you approach the waterfall, you will see the affects of the fire to the terrain. You turn left at this junction, and proceed to follow all trail signs directing you to both the TRT and the waterfall.

Over this 0.7-mile section, you will gain another 386', but you can take many breaks along this section to take advantage of the views. This is a popular trail for tourists, but the hikers are extremely friendly and good sports about moving aside for the speedier ones. There is a bridge at the waterfall that flows into Edgewood Creek and water access for your pooch.

The bridge is a good turnaround spot, or if you wish, you can continue another 2.2 miles to the TRT junction, climbing an additional 700'. From this junction, you can proceed in either direction to walk along the TRT for as far as you would like, or visit another photo spot at a scenic vista another 0.4 miles along the trail. If you decide to turn around after the waterfall, definitely take the spur trail to the overlook on your return. It is a mere two minute side trip, a climb of only 70', and you will have another great view of Lake Tahoe. Just below the tallest boulders here, a flat area invites you to enjoy your lunch before returning to your vehicle.

Share with: Equestrians, mountain bikers, bird watchers

19 – Tahoe Rim Trail to Cinder Cone
Tahoe City
Tahoe National Forest

Difficulty: 2
Distance: 3.0 miles
Elevation: 630' gain (6500' elevation)

Directions: Coming from the direction of South Lake Tahoe on Highway 89 (at the "Y" where Highway 50 veers to the right, you stay straight to continue on Highway 89 toward Tahoe City), drive 27.3 miles into Tahoe City. Here you turn left in the direction of Squaw Valley. Choose the outside lane turning left here. Just 0.1 miles after the left turn, you make a right onto Fairway Drive. Drive 0.3 miles up Fairway to find the trailhead for the Tahoe Rim Trail on your left. There is room for about three cars to park here, but you can park legally across the street in the Community Center's paved parking lot.

Coming from I-80, take Exit 185 in the direction of Squaw Valley, Tahoe City, and Lake Tahoe. Then travel 13.5 miles on Highway 89 to the left turn onto Fairway Drive.

Description: One word best describes this trail, and it is the "views." Be sure to bring along a camera to capture the great scenes of Lake Tahoe, Tahoe City, distant snow-capped peaks, and the lava cliffs resulting from a cinder cone volcano. Also, bring along water for your dog since the seasonal streams are unpredictable and the destination is to rock formations rather than the usual alpine lake.

Starting from the trailhead, you climb steadily uphill for 20 minutes, gaining 360'. Soon your reward is some great views out to Lake Tahoe, with peaks bordering its far shore, and boats in its deep, blue water. Each turn on this section of trail offers a new scene for photographing.

Early wildflowers also dot the landscape, with the abundant yellow sidesaddle goldenrod dominating, along with some early mule ears, and newly emerging deep red snow plants. This is such an enjoyable part of the trail, with its easy grade, and the sense you have of walking along the rim of the world. Your trail takes you through hills of brush, notably manzanita, but also enough firs and cedars to keep you shaded. There are two crossings past fire roads, but you want to remain on the narrower footpath at each intersection. If you look ahead of you on the trail, you will see the blue Tahoe Rim Trail logo sign nailed above eye level on a tree to help direct you.

Soon you cross a small stream and then start another small climb. More trees replace the brush, with the trail taking you through a forested area, and eventually a couple more streams (these will likely be dry by the end of the month). Temporarily, you are without any great views, but then at the 3-mile mark, you emerge from the forest to glimpse distant lava rock formations.

You reach your Cinder Cone destination as the trail starts to veer to the right. At Cinder Cone, you can find a nice shady, flat spot for a picnic. You have great views across to peaks, KT-22 (8,070') and Silver Peak (8,424'). Below, you can see the Truckee River and Highway 89 making its way to Squaw Valley. Be careful on the loose rocks and steep drop off.

At Cinder Cone, you are truly at the edge of the cliff. From here, the trail continues on to Painted Rocks (another 6.0 miles) and Watson Lake (an additional 4.5 miles), but this is a good turnaround point for a day hike.

Share with: Bikers (this is a great mountain bike trail) and equestrians.

Did you know? The Tahoe Rim Trail covers 165 miles high above Lake Tahoe, with nine trailheads comprising the trail system. Hikers, joggers, and equestrians are allowed on the entire loop, and mountain bikes are allowed on portions with some restrictions. Visit **www.tahoerimtrail. org** for more information.

20 – Caples Creek Trail
Kyburz, CA

Difficulty: 2

Distance: 3.85 miles to Government Meadows (about two hours to end of trail)

Elevation: This is an uphill hike, gaining 730', including one 225' ascent

Directions: On Highway 50 in Kyburz, look for the "Silverfork Road 1 Mile" sign. Turn right onto Silverfork Road and proceed 9.0 miles to the trailhead on your left (0.5 mile past Silver Fork Campground). If you cross the Fitch Rantz Bridge over the Silver Fork of the American River, then you have just passed the trailhead. There is plenty of parking here. At 5,000' elevation, you can get to this trail in May unless it has been a heavy or late snow year. To verify Silverfork Road is open, call the Placerville Ranger District at (530) 644-2324 (or visit www.fs.fed.us/r5/eldorado).

Description: This is a good family hike, not too difficult, and a lot of variety in terrain and ecosystems to enjoy. In May, you may encounter snow patches and a lot of water on the trail, especially through the meadows (unless it was a light snow year). You will see bright red cactus-like succulent snow plants along the creek, along with alders and willows. The trail is forested, with large cedar, aspen, and Jeffrey pines, and an occasional oak with its fresh new leaves.

Start up the dirt road from the parking area to reach the trailhead marked as 17E51. Within 10 minutes of this hike, you will reach Caples Creek and a great view of it cascading down rocky steps. Here the trail takes off to the left up the hill (at one time a post marked this junction). Now there are no markings to follow, but you can discern the dirt path. In another 20 minutes, you will reach a beautiful waterfall, the outlet flow from Caples Lake.

Continuing on the trail, you will find that the waters below calm and pool, enhancing some beach areas along the creek for resting or picnicking. At 1.2 miles along the trail, you will encounter a marker post, indicating Government Meadows straight ahead and Silver Fork to the right. For a quick side trip, take the fork to the right to find a bridge crossing Caples Creek, a stunning view to the water below, and a possible alternate trail option for the Silver Fork Trail.

Within one hour of your trek, you are at the first of four meadows. For the less ambitious, there are plenty of options for stopping and for everyone else the trail continues to the destination of Government Meadows, making for a 7.7-mile round trip adventure. Continuing on to Government Meadows, you are treated to stunning rock formations and towering big trees. As you enter a second meadow, look to your left to see an impressive crag above you. Beware here as we have often spotted a bear in this meadow. If you have a tenacious dog, be sure to keep it leashed through the meadows. A post in the third meadow is signed Jake Schnieder. A spur trail takes you to the creek, a pleasant lunch spot, and a possible low water crossing to connect you to the Silver Fork Trail.

Return from the spur to the main trail and continue straight through Jake Schnieder Meadow another 0.8 miles toward Hay Flat before coming to a final post indicating Government Meadows to your right. Turn here to find the fourth (and least impressive) meadow. Continue past the meadow another 0.25 mile to the trail's end at the creek and find a nice lunch spot. While there is loop trail available and mapped on the trailhead kiosk, it is difficult to follow and involves two water crossings, so I suggest you return on the same trail.

If you revisit here in October, you will enjoy a display of fall colors. If you are adventuresome, you can find the trail after the bridge across Caples Creek that starts you on the Silver Fork Loop. You follow the trail uphill for the first 1.4 miles, climbing along the descending American River. Once you crest, the next 1.5 miles are gently undulating, rich in foliage and water access spots. The kiosk suggests a loop for you to do here, but I do not suggest going any further beyond the 2.9 miles described above. Other trail junctions can be confusing, and we have never found a safe way to cross the water at Government Meadows. We have successfully crossed at Jake Schneider, however, so if you wish to try that loop be sure to take a picture of the trail map to take with you on this 8.1-mile adventure. I would do that loop in a clockwise direction to verify the water crossing at Jake Schneider is safe to try.

Share with: Equestrians

Less Ambitious: Stop at either China Flat or Silver Fork Campground for wildlife viewing. Expect to see eagles, ducks and geese, as well as chipmunks, squirrels, and deer. Then walk along the Caples Creek Trail for about 30 minutes before turning around.

21 – Lover's Leap
Camp Sacramento

Difficulty: 2
Distance: 1.4 miles from parking area to Lover's Leap
Elevation: 500' ascent (steepest last 0.4 mile)

Directions: From Strawberry on Highway 50, continue another 3.0 miles east to Camp Sacramento on your right. Turn into the camp on the dirt road and just past the bridge find the Lover's Leap Trail parking on your left. There is space for about six vehicles here. Do not park in the campground or in the area to the right after the bridge, since this is reserved for campers at the resort. If the parking area is full, you can return to Highway 50 and find a large turnout you can use and then walk into the camp.

Description: Your first view of Lover's Leap will be in Strawberry. Look up to the right to see its sheer face. The hike from here would be imposing, but by driving another 3.0 miles up the highway, the hike from Camp Sacramento is less of a trek.

From the parking area, walk up the dirt road into the camp. Walk past the camp store, heading in the direction of Strawberry. Just beyond Cabin 52, you will find the Lover's Leap trailhead (0.15 mile from the parking area). The first part of the walk is through a shaded riparian forest of alders, aspen, and pines, along with native brush and a wide selection of wildflowers. Within 0.25 mile, you will arrive at a series of streams. There are also two side trails marked with XP posts, designating cross-country trails. The first of these points is to your left and the second one is to the right. In both cases, continue straight to remain on the Lover's Leap trail. A few minutes beyond the streams, stop and look out across the canyon for a great view of Horsetail Falls.

After a mile of leisurely strolling, you will have easily gained 250 feet. You will gain the remaining 250 feet in the next 0.4 mile. This portion of the trail leaves the shade and you will start climbing over rocks, switch backing your way up the grade. At points, the trail becomes confusing with faint spurs to distract you. You need to look ahead to find the more well traveled path and stick to it. When you feel a need to stop for a rest, take in the spectacular views. You are almost to the top now, with the remaining part less strenuous. When you arrive, you will see a sign on a tree to mark Lover's Leap. In addition, the sign reminds you **DO NOT THROW ROCKS** over the side, since rock climbers frequent the area and rocks could kill them.

While the hike up to the summit may have been a heart- throb, the rewarding views are well worth the effort. Take time to look around at the 360-degree sites, including 9983' Pyramid Peak and 9235' Ralston Peak. Look down to Highway 50 and Strawberry. Do not go too close to the edge and do not allow children to run around, with an obvious danger to an accidental fall. When you are ready to leave, be sure to return on the trail that you arrived on. Another trail down is also available, but this one will take you down to Strawberry and it would be a long walk back to your car. To be safe, make a note of your return route as soon as you arrive.

JUNE

In June, you can usually reach some mountain trails, while others may still be laden with patches of snow. If too much snow remains, it may delay your getting access to the trail to Forni Lake. The highlight of this hike is the display of fields of mule ears in bloom, usually at their height around Father's Day. If snow delays access to the trail then most likely the bloom will be later also.

Field of mule ears on trail to Forni Lake

22 – Bay View Campground Trails
Highway 89 – Emerald Bay

A visit to the Bay View Campground trails off Highway 89 near Emerald Bay offers two hiking possibilities – one to a popular waterfall, and the other to a stunning alpine lake. If you are up to the more strenuous climb to the lake, then choose the hike to Granite Lake. For the easier option, choose the hike to the waterfall. You can also consider doing both hikes in one visit. The hike to the falls is family-friendly, but your dog will need to remain leashed for this outing. If anyone in your group has problems with knees, be aware that you have to climb numerous rock steps to reach the waterfall. This may be problematic for a senior dog also.

Directions: At the "Y" in South Lake Tahoe, where Highway 50 splits to the right away from Highway 89, stay straight, remaining on Highway 89 in the direction of Tahoe City. Travel 7.7 miles to the Bay View Campground on the left. Drive through the campground to the designated parking area and the trailhead. There is space for about 20 cars here, but if the area is full, you can return to the highway to find additional spaces. Do not park in the equestrian parking area or in the campground sites. This is an extremely popular tourist site, so consider a mid-week outing.

Cascade Creek Fall Trail

Difficulty: 2
Distance: 0.8 miles to head of waterfall
Elevation: 50' ascent and then 115' descent to falls

Description: This is a short hike to a spectacular waterfall. You will want to do Cascade Creek Fall Trail as soon as the snowmelt permits to avoid the inevitable crowds later in the season. The trail is easy to follow, but difficult to traverse due to its many rocky steps. It can be very sunny on the trail, and very dusty. Be sure to pack sun hats and plenty of water. If you have balance issues, then this hike is not appropriate for you. The trail is narrow, so you should hike it slowly and carefully. You need good trail shoes to avoid slipping. I have seen many hikers here with scraped knees. From the parking area, you start just beyond the trail's kiosk. You do not need a Wilderness Permit since the falls are not within Desolation's boundary. At the start of the trail, you see the sign pointing you to the left for Cascade Falls. The trail starts out easily on a nice dirt footpath. Soon you start a small 50' ascent on rocky steps. You can look down to Cascade Lake below, and to Lake Tahoe in the distance. At 0.5 miles, you have a great view of the falls in the distance. This is a possible turnaround point if you are new to exercise.

Continuing on the trail, you start a careful 115-foot descent. At 0.75 miles, you can look down to your left to see a wood post. The post marks a trail to the left down to the falls, or a trail straight ahead to the creek. You want to take the trail down to the falls to reach the headwaters. From that vantage point, you have some awesome photography opportunities. You must maintain caution at all times, because a fall could be fatal. Do not allow children or dogs too close to the edge.

After photographing the falls, you can proceed to the creek. Here dogs and kids can play more safely. You do not need to cross the creek in order to view the falls. Take time to rest at the creek before your return trip. On this leg of the hike, you have the 115' ascent ahead of you. Take your time, and when you reach the flat forest portion toward the end, try a little bird watching. The group in front of us spotted a golden-crowned kinglet.

After the hike, return to Camp Richardson and walk around town. There is a bike trail, with both paved and dirt options. You can stop for an ice cream cone and sit out on the lawn with your pooch in the shade. You can make this into a nice family day trip.

Bay View Trail
Granite Lake

Difficulty: 3
Distance: 1.1 miles to the lake
Elevation: 800'

Directions: Parking for the Bay View Trail is the same as for the Cascade Creek Fall hike. From the parking area, visit the trail's kiosk and fill out a Day Use Permit for hiking into Desolation Wilderness. The trail starts to the right of the kiosk.

Description: With it only being 1.1 miles to Granite Lake, one would not expect a difficulty rating of '3', but it is a strenuous 800' uphill climb over the short distance, making it seem much longer than it actually is. Do this hike as early in the season as it opens to avoid summer's heat later and the expected increased amount of other hikers. The path is dry and exposed in sections, while other sections are shaded and cooler. There may be remaining snow patches along the upper sections.

At 0.4 miles, you will come to the Desolation Wilderness sign and a small stream crossing. This is immediately followed by a rock lookout with great vistas down to Cascade Lake, Lake Tahoe, Fannette Island, Emerald Bay, the distant Sierras, and Lake Tahoe's many sandy beaches. While this first part of the trail may be dusty and dry, there are sufficient switchbacks and ample shade to minimize the difficulty. At 0.5 miles, another lookout follows with views down toward Vikingsholm (the castle itself is shrouded in trees). You have climbed 461' at this point. With luck, a gentle breeze may pick up to cool you.

The trail now climbs away from Lake Tahoe and into a pine grove of Lodgepole and fir. Portions follow along the stream from Granite Lake's outflow and here you will find alder and willows typical of a riparian environment. At 1.0 miles, you crest at the high point along the trail and get your first views of Granite Lake. From here, follow a ducked path 0.1 miles down to the lake.

Granite Lake

Granite Lake's southern edge is framed by the 8699' Maggie's Peak – the taller of the two peaks named Maggie's Peaks. You can enjoy a relaxing break here at the lake and try fishing for brook trout, or consider an additional hike up to the saddle between the two peaks. This will involve another strenuous 800' climb to reach the panoramic view down to Emerald Bay and Lake Tahoe. Expect to encounter patches of ice during the 0.5-mile climb, and bring trekking poles and crampons for your boots to pass safely through these sections. The trail continues downhill from here to join with the Velma Lakes Trail or a possible loop trail down to Eagle Lake and Upper Eagle Falls. To accomplish the 5.4-mile loop, you would need a second car parked at the Eagle Falls trailhead. I would suggest doing the loop in a counterclockwise direction, starting at Eagle Falls and ending at Bay View so you do not drop down from Maggie's Peaks only to risk discovering snow blocking the rest of the loop and face having to climb the peak again.

23 – Horsetail Falls
Pyramid Creek Trail
Twin Bridges, CA

Difficulty: 2+
Distance: 1.5 miles to the waterfall
Elevation: 760' gain

Directions: From Highway 50 East, about 11 miles beyond Kyburz in Twin Bridges, find the parking area for Pyramid Creek on your left. There is a center turn lane here just after a passing lane and just prior to the bridge crossing Pyramid Creek. There is a parking fee ($5.00 in 2016).

Description: Horsetail Falls are beautiful, loud, and photographic. The trail, however, is difficult to follow, poorly marked, and not maintained, probably due to injuries suffered by hikers trying to go beyond the foot of the falls and climbing the slippery rocks to the top. You will not get lost, because on the hike up you can both see and hear the falls to give you direction. Coming back down, whatever path you take should take you back to Highway 50. Nevertheless, the hike is a tracking challenge and you may need to be happy with however far you make it.

Ideally, you want to go as soon as the snow melts, the paths and rocks have dried, and the streams lowered – you want optimum water volume with the falls, with as little water on the trail as possible. Generally, this is a great hike for June.

From the parking area, be sure to pay the day use fee before starting out on the trail. Within minutes, you will be at Pyramid Creek where the trail veers to the left, keeping the creek on your right. Continue along the creek until you reach a trail sign pointing you to the left. The trail returns to follow the creek most of the way, always with the creek on your right. Misleading spur trails abound to steer you to the creek, but remember your goal is to go uphill to the falls.

Follow the trail posts pointing in the direction of the Wilderness Boundary. After about 0.5 mile, the trail ends at the base of a large rock slab. You must hike directly up the granite wall to rejoin the actual trail. When your climb finally plateaus, you will get your first view of the falls in the distance. If you turn around, you will have a great view of Lover's Leap looking back in the direction of Highway 50.

After about 0.75 mile, you will enter Desolation Wilderness. There is a kiosk toward the left with day use permits to fill out. The trail continues directly from the kiosk on the right of the sign. The trail takes you along a cool creek and welcoming shade. You may have to get your feet a little wet in a heavy snow season; otherwise, the crossings will be relatively easy. You will come to one area where you walk along a ledge skirting a small pond – yes, this is the trail. Later the trail takes you seemingly under a large rock.

You then walk up rocks toward the falls. At the last part, you hike up a gully to the trail's end at the base of the falls. Do not attempt to go any further than this, and keep dogs away from the steep trail edges. It is too easy to slip on the flat rocks to attempt an approach to the edge. The gully is safely away from the edge, but the rocks are still slippery and you can easily end up on your bottom. Use your hands to hold on to other rocks and ensure your balance. Wear hiking boots with good tread for this trek.

Making it to the base is rewarding and worth any mental or physical struggles. On your way down, do not be surprised if you cannot follow the exact way you came up! We never seem to return the same way we arrived. This hike is definitely a challenge, but the distance is not great, the climb not too difficult, and the rewards well worth it. Just employ caution throughout your journey to insure yours and your dog's safety.

24 – Spider and Buck Island Lakes
Loon Lake Trail
Ice House Road

Difficulty: 3 (for distance)
Distance: 3.6 miles to Pleasant Campground junction
4.5 miles to spurs to Spider Lake
5.9 miles to Buck Island Lake
Elevation: 360' climb to Spider Lake; 287' descent to Buck Island Lake

Warning: Depending on the winter season, the Forest Service may not have opened the road to the free Wilderness Parking. If you have to park in the Loon Lake Boat Launch area, you may need to pay a parking fee ($7.00 in 2010). You would also need to add 0.5 mile to your hiking distance if you park here. Call the Pacific Ranger District at (530) 647-5415 to verify if parking is open for the season.

Directions: Heading East on Highway 50, take the Ice House Road Exit on your left in the direction of Crystal Basin Recreation Area (about 22 miles east of Placerville). Follow Ice House Road 24.3 miles to a right turn to Loon Lake. Proceed 4.5 miles to the entrance to Loon Lake Campground. Drive into the campground and follow signs to Wilderness Parking. The parking area is quite large and has toilet facilities. Day passes are available at the trailhead; however, you will not need one to hike into Buck Island Lake since it is outside the Desolation Wilderness boundary. If you plan to continue past Buck Island to Rockbound Lake (another 0.6 miles), then you will need a wilderness pass. This early in the season, you may want to stop at the Mill Run Ranger Station in Fresh Pond for your pass in case the kiosk area is not stocked yet.

Description: Your dog is going to love this hike in El Dorado National Forest, with three lakes to splash in, many streams to cross, and open spaces to explore. Dispose of any garbage from your drive in the large dumpster at the trailhead. Do not leave any food items, a cooler in sight, or even a stick of gum in your car or you may risk a bear breaking in and ravaging it.

The Loon Lake Trail starts at a 6280' elevation and climbs only 360', making it usually doable in June after the snowmelt. Making this hike early in the season will take advantage of cooler weather for a six-mile outing. You will also encounter fewer people on the trail at this time. On the down side, there will be numerous water crossings to make, involving rock hopping, and the trail will probably have fallen trees to get past since the forest service will not have done trail maintenance yet. Be very careful with the water crossings, and try to go around trees rather than climbing over them to avoid inadvertent injuries from broken branches.

The Loon Lake Trail parallels the lake, so you should be able to discern the main trail from the spurs leading uphill away from the lake, or others that are simply taking you down to the lake's shore. The first 2.5 miles afford you views of Loon Lake and its distant peaks. On your right, Brown Mountain looms at 7144'. Across the lake, you can see Guide Peak at 7741'. Along the trail itself, manzanita is in full bloom with its pink flowers, and numerous rock outcroppings abound, including large, distinguished boulders.

At 3.1 miles, the trail turns away from the lake in order to travel in toward a gully for an easier water crossing. After traversing the gully, the trail veers back toward Loon Lake. Then the trail widens into a rocky uphill road for a 0.5-mile climb. Halfway, you plateau and can stop to look across Loon Lake to its dam, and down to the Pleasant Lake portion of the larger Loon Lake. There is a boat-in campground at Pleasant Lake. At the 3.6-mile mark, there is a signed junction with a 0.4-mile trail taking you down to the campground. For an easier hike, you can consider this your turnaround spot.

Curry playing at Loon Lake

For those continuing on to Spider Lake, the trail turns away from Loon Lake at this point. You walk on a rocky jeep road (no longer open to motorized vehicles), once known as the Rubicon Trail. At about 4.5 miles, you can look to the left for glimpses of Spider Lake below. You start to see some "ducks" marking access routes down to the lake. There are no very clear routes, but you can still easily make your way down with the lake's direction in clear view. For 0.25 miles, you continue to see Spider Lake below, and additional "ducks" marking possible routes. Appropriately-named Spider Lake has many spider-like arms.

After your stay at Spider Lake, return to the main trail and continue in the direction of Buck Island Lake. You descend 287' over a mile of trail. At the 5.9-mile point of your hike, the jeep trail ends at Buck Island Lake, named for the island in its center. Looking straight across the lake, you can see the incoming cascades of water. Looking to your left, you can see the lake's dam and the Wentworth Jeep Trail. Enjoy your rest at Buck Island, watching the small, illusive fish jump.

Remember that you have a long hike back to your car. Give yourself at least three hours for each direction. If you are short on time, or energy, you can stop the hike at Pleasant Campground, or Spider Lake, and still have a great outing.

More Ambitious: While the old jeep trail ends at Buck Island Lake, a foot trail continues from there. In 0.6 miles, you reach Rockbound Lake. If you are considering this extra hiking, then you will need to pick up a Day Use Permit at the trailhead (or in Fresh Pond at the Mill Run Ranger Station), since Rockbound Lake is within Desolation Wilderness.

Share with: Equestrians.

25 – Forni Lake
Highland Trail
Crystal Basin Recreation Area

Difficulty:	3 to Wilderness Boundary; 4 to lake
Distance:	3.8 miles to Wilderness Boundary
	4.5 miles to Forni Lake
Elevation:	1390' overall gain with
	470' first 3.2 miles (moderate)
	920' gain last 1.4 miles (steep)

Warning: *You walk through meadows and marshes on this hike, so carry and apply ample bug spray and have spare socks available. Call the ranger at 530-647-5415 to verify Cheese Camp Road is clear of snow before attempting the drive.*

Directions: Stop in Fresh Pond at the Mill Run Ranger Station along Highway 50 to pick up your Day Use Permit to enter Desolation Wilderness if planning to hike the entire trail to Forni Lake. This is early in the season, so you may not find passes available at the trailhead parking.

Exit Highway 50 at Ice House Road to enter the Crystal Basin Recreation Area (this is a left turn about 22 miles east of Placerville and 5.0 miles east of Fresh Pone). Travel on Ice House Road for 20.7 miles and turn right (east) onto Cheese Camp Road (Road 36) in the direction of Van Vleck Ranch and the Desolation Wilderness Trailhead. Drive 5.4 miles on paved Cheese Camp Road to the locked gate at Tells Creek. The trail starts just beyond the gate. Do not block the gate with your car.

If there is no room to park along the roadside here, return 500' to a dirt road on the left and proceed 0.1 miles to a larger parking area. This is the parking area for the Van Vleck Trailhead. Later in the season, there is a kiosk for Desolation Wilderness with Day Use Permits here, and a map of the trails in this area. In late June, you can expect no signage or permits here, but there are facilities open further inside the campground area.

If you park in the Van Vleck Trailhead parking area, just walk back to Cheese Camp Road and the Tells Creek gate to start your hike. Distances are from the service gate.

If you are coming from the Georgetown area, then look at the suggestion for the return trip route for your initial drive here.

Description: The majority of this hike (3.8 miles) is moderate, with a very gradual climb. You walk through numerous meadows of wildflowers, past many streams, and through a fir and pine forest. You enjoy distant views of peaks, with McConnell Peak ahead of you standing at 9099'. Depending on the winter season's rain and snow, you may have some marshy sections in the meadows to deal with. Do carry plenty of mosquito spray with you for this meadow adventure in El Dorado National Forest.

Starting from the locked gate, walk on a dirt service road (unfortunately marred from a 2009 fire) for 0.7 miles to a trail intersection. Two trails take off from this intersection, with the one to the right going to the Red Peak Trail, and the one to the left going to Loon Lake. Stay straight at this intersection and continue on the service road. In another 0.6 miles, you find the signed Highland Trail to your right, starting from a weather station for measuring snow also on your right.

Take the trail on the right, leaving the service road to start the Highland Trail. This is a well-marked trail with numerous posts directing you along your path. In marshy areas where you may need to leave the trail temporarily, posts ahead redirect you to the correct path.

After 1.8 miles on the Highland Trail, you come to an intersection with the Shadow Lake Trail. Stay on the Highland Trail to your right. From here, it is just 0.7 miles, but a 257' climb, to the Desolation Wilderness Boundary sign. If you do not want to do the next leg of the hike (more difficult portion), then stop here at the sign, have your lunch, and return to your car.

For those continuing on to Forni Lake, you now face a 663' climb over the next 0.7 miles. Fortunately, this journey is in two sections, first a 313' ascent to the Forni Lake outlet stream. During this difficult stretch, take a break and look backwards down to Loon Lake in the distance. The trail flattens here where you need to cross the stream. Then the next steep section starts with another 350' gully climb along the lake's outlet waters. When you peak, you can see the lake just below you.

Fishing is good at Forni Lake, with eastern brook and golden trout. Be careful going down the gully on your return trip, since the rocks are loose in places and it would be easy to slip.

For your return drive, consider a route to Georgetown to avoid the late afternoon Placerville traffic common on Highway 50. To go this way, return on Cheese Camp Road to Ice House Road and turn right for 2.0 miles to a left turn onto Wentworth Springs Road. If you want a fun stop along your route before reaching Georgetown, drive 18.6 miles on Wentworth Springs and locate the sign for Uncle Tom's Cabin on the left. The road soon becomes a dirt path, but it is only about one minute before you reach dog-friendly Uncle Tom's Cabin. You can purchase a soda or beer in the can and sit inside the quaint campground bar decorated with dollar bills, or enjoy your refreshments outdoors on the deck with your dog. Return to Wentworth Springs to continue the drive to Georgetown another 11.4 miles.

In Georgetown, you may want to stop to stroll down Main Street to visit some of its unique establishments before continuing home. From Georgetown, you can choose to take Highway 193 left (south) in the direction of Placerville, travel straight to Lower Main Street and onto Marshall Road in the direction of Garden Valley and Coloma, or take Highway 193 right (north) in the direction of Auburn. If one of these directions takes you close to your destination, then this will be an enjoyable option for your drive home.

Share with: Equestrians and mountain bikes (bikes only allowed on the first 2.6 miles of the trail up to the junction with the Shadow Lake Trail).

26 – Salmon and Loch Leven Lakes
Tahoe National Forest

Difficulty: 2
Distance: 1.4 miles to Salmon Lake
Another 0.9 miles to Upper Loch Leven Lake
Then 0.2 miles to Lower Loch Leven
Another 0.8 miles to High Loch Leven
Round trip to all four lakes, 6.0 miles
Elevation: Rolling, with 250' overall gain, consisting of numerous 20-100' ups and downs

Directions: Take Exit 160 on I-80 for Yuba Gap (about 40 miles east of Auburn). Turn south (right if coming from Auburn direction) on Yuba Gap for 0.2 miles and turn right in the direction of Lodgepole Campground. Continue another 1.1 miles and turn left onto Road 19 (not signed) in the direction of Silvertip. Drive 4.0 miles on Road 19 (do not follow the later turn toward Silvertip) and turn left onto Road 38. Drive 1.9 miles, past Huysink Lake, to the trailhead for Salmon Lake and parking areas along the roadside.

Warning: *Road 19 and Road 38 are both rough, dirt roads.*

Description: This is a well-signed, easy hike to four alpine lakes, requiring only moderate trail-reading skills. This is an excellent opportunity to study trails before trying the ones more difficult to follow in Desolation Wilderness. Give yourself plenty of time to visit each lake along the way.

The trail starts with budding willows and a small meadow full of wildflowers. You then slowly rise and hike through a forest of pines and firs. You emerge from the forest, skirt by a pond, and peak at a point with great views of mountain peaks, including an impressive half-face one. From the summit, you can venture to your right and gain an overhead view down to Salmon Lake. Keeping to the trail, you descend at the end of the first mile to a junction sign

At the junction, go to the right in the direction of Salmon Lake, an easy 0.3 miles ahead. The lake offers some great views of distant mountains, and (surprisingly) schools of catfish in its waters. You can make your way to the opposite shore by walking around in a clockwise direction. Salmon Lake will be the least popular of the lakes you visit on this hike, so enjoy its solitude.

After your stay at Salmon Lake, return the 0.3 miles to the trail junction and take the other arm to Loch Leven Lakes. In 0.6 miles, you reach Upper Loch Leven Lake and another trail junction. Go right here to reach Lower and High Loch Leven Lakes. Lower Loch Leven is just 0.2 miles beyond the first lake.

At Lower Loch Leven, you find numerous islands inviting you for a swim (probably better swimming in another month). The trail goes 0.3 miles along the lake, and at the far end, you reach a junction signed for Cherry Point to the right. Stay left here, and it is another 0.5 miles to High Loch Leven Lake.

This is a great starting hike for the summer season. You will find the trail mostly a dirt footpath and easy to follow. The more difficult sections over rocks are marked in places with painted swaths on large rocks, ribbons in trees, and "ducks". If you find following the trail worrisome or difficult, then you may not enjoy later hikes in Desolation

Wilderness. Take time honing your reading skills here to gain confidence for the later hikes.

27 - Tamarack, Ralston, and Cagwin Lakes
Echo Lakes Trail

Difficulty: 2
Distance: 4.1 miles to lakes
Elevation: 380' gain

Directions: Heading East on Highway 50, continue 6.0 miles beyond Twin Bridges, making a left onto Johnson Pass Road. Drive 0.5 mile to a left onto Echo Lakes Road. Continue 1.0 mile down Echo Lakes to the large parking area above the resort. There is both a paved and a dirt parking area. A trail down to the resort starts from the dirt parking lot, signed on a tree. You walk steeply down the trail (100-foot descent in 0.15 mile) to reach the resort.

Description: Starting at the resort, walk across the dam to a kiosk with day use permits. From here, climb a short distance to a plateau with a trail coming in on the right. Your Echo Lakes Trail heads to the left here to parallel Lower and Upper Echo Lakes for 2.5 miles. This part of the hike is relatively flat, with little rolling hills and one switchback. While you hike, you can look down on the summer lake homes with envy. When you leave the lakes behind, you continue another 0.6 mile to reach the boundary for Desolation Wilderness. From here, continue another 0.5 mile to a post on your left signed for Tamarack Lake.

Tamarack Lake

The trail down to Tamarack is a short 0.25 mile and a little vague at times. When you reach the lake, be sure to note trail signs for your return trip. Tamarack is the largest of the three lakes in the Ralston Peak basin, also the most popular to visit. To leave the crowds, continue on the trail along the lake's eastern shore. In a short distance, it moves away from the lake and then climbs up to your left over some rocks. When you reach the top, you can look down to see Ralston Lake below. Ralston is 0.2 mile from Tamarack Lake.

At Ralston, you can cross its rock dam to reach its eastern shore with nice sandy beach areas. The water is deep and perfect for swimming or fishing. On the western shore, there are large boulders at the water's edge. Ralston is a very pretty lake with a view up to Ralston Peak at its southern end.

After your stay at Ralston, continue a short 0.1 mile to Cagwin Lake. To reach Cagwin, you head away from Ralston from its dam end to find the trail. In a short distance, you will see Cagwin Lake down to your right. Cagwin is the smallest of the three lakes, but more secluded with fewer visitors. Not as deep as Ralston, there is more vegetation in the water. From Cagwin Lake, return to Ralston and then to Tamarack for your trip home.

Less Ambitious Option: Plan to do this hike before Labor Day and take the water taxi at the Echo Lakes Resort. This cuts out the first 2.5 miles of the hike. The taxi costs $14.00/person and $5.00/dog one-way (2016 prices). Call ahead for times (530) 659-7207. The taxi does not run after Labor Day Weekend and will only operate with a minimum of three paying riders.

July

Mosquitoes are abundant, but so are the wildflowers – so bring your repellant and your camera for some great hikes in the mountains. Summer days are cooler at the higher elevations, and you escape the crowds, rattlesnakes, and star thistle populating trails in the foothills.

View approaching Shealor Lake

28 – Shealor Lake
Highway 88 near Silver Lake

Difficulty: 2
Distance: 1 mile to lake
Elevation: 238' climb from trailhead on route to lake; 470' climb out from lake

Directions: From Highway 50 in Pollock Pines, take Exit 60 for Sly Park Road. When you exit the freeway, take a right onto Sly Park Road and continue 4.6 miles. Make a left onto Mormon Emigrant Trail and go about 25 miles to its end at Highway 88. Make a left and head east on 88 for 5.7 miles and locate the Shealor Lake Trailhead parking on your left. Coming from the Lake Tahoe area, take Highway 89 South in Meyers 11.0 miles to its end at Highway 88. Turn right here and drive westward on Highway 88 to the trailhead entrance on the right 11.6 miles beyond the Carson Pass Ranger Station.

Description: Although this is a short hike, the hike in is slow, taking about 45 minutes one-way. The trail starts with a climb of 238' on a well-marked path. At the top of the climb, you can enjoy the great views before starting the 470' drop to the lake on a very rocky path. Take your time on the descent to be sure of your footing on the loose rocks. Also, look carefully for the trail markings, such as the rock piled "ducks" and other hiker's footprints.

This is a very pretty hike with views of your destination lake early in your descent. Seeing the lake early on fooled our son, Jake, on his first attempt at this hike, and he just started down toward it, leaving the trail and making for a difficult descent down rocks. So do not let its sighting lure you off-trail. Stay focused and you will safely make it down. When you arrive at the bottom, make a mental note of where the trail emerges for your return trip.

The lake itself has nice clear water for swimming. You can walk around to its eastern shore and see numerous campsites for backpackers.

You can also venture from the lake and find a pond beyond it (visible on your hike in to the lake).

The return 470' climb is not as difficult as you would anticipate, as there are many switchbacks making for an easy ascent. With the higher elevations and cooler temperatures in the Kirkwood area, this is a good destination on a hot summer afternoon to escape the heat at lower elevations.

29 – Enchanted Pools
Wrights Lake Recreation Area
El Dorado National Forest

Difficulty: 2
Distance: 1.75 miles
Elevation: 700' gain, very gradual and easy

Before the hike: Stop for breakfast at the Greenhouse Café in Placerville. Take Exit 44B on Highway 50, signed for Forni Road. Follow the exit road and cross back over the freeway onto Placerville Drive. Drive about 0.5 miles, first passing the fairgrounds, and then the Raley's shopping center. Make a right onto Ray Lawyer Drive at the light just beyond Raley's. Turn into the shopping center on the right at the El Dorado Savings Bank. The café is in the buildings between Raley's and the bank. Dogs are welcome in their outdoor patio area. (530) 626-4081

Directions: Head East on Highway 50 and travel 4.8 miles beyond Kyburz, and turn left onto Wrights Road. Travel 8.1 miles on Wrights Road to the campground. You first pass the overflow parking area and then reach a Stop sign. At the Stop, turn right and go 1.0 mile to the Twin Lakes Trailhead parking area. The trailhead and Day Use Permit kiosk are just below the parking area beyond the service gate. If the popular parking area is full, then you need to return to the overflow lot and walk in the additional 1.0 mile.

Description: This is a non-maintained and unofficial route to access Desolation Wilderness. If you are not comfortable using an unofficial trail, then you should not attempt this hike. This is a popular hike for the Wrights Lake cabin owners, so you will be able to follow the footsteps of others at times. The areas across the rock slabs are more difficult to follow, but your path is generally in a straight line.

The Enchanted Pools are formed by the confluence of the outlet flows from Umpa Lake and Lower Twin Lake, providing a destination well worth any effort. Why there is no official route to the pools is hard to understand. The upper pool is like an alpine lake and lush with waterfalls filling its small frame. Before you reach the lake, you hike past other falls and pools of water, all making for great resting spots, swimming holes, and fishing opportunities.

Starting from the trailhead, start on the Loop Trail, signed Twin & Grouse Lake Trail. After 0.4 miles, you depart the Loop Trail and head right in the signed direction for "Twin Lakes Island Grouse Hemlock Smith." You are going to hike just 0.1 miles on this trail and then strike out to your left on a straight plane (use a pedometer to measure the 0.1 miles). Look straight ahead on that plane for your first "ducks" to confirm your path. The "ducks" may be sparse or misplaced intentionally by the cabin owners. There is also a footpath leading downhill to confuse you. Try to stay on a straight, level path across the rock slabs.

After 0.15 miles on this path, you pick up an obvious dirt trail taking you down and across the Grouse Lake outlet stream with its beautiful waterfall. After crossing the creek (this can be very slippery), your trail over the next 0.33 miles continually switches between dirt paths in small pine groves, and then undefined treks across rock slabs. At one point, the trail takes you around a very large rock, and empties you into a rock valley. There appears to be a path straight ahead of you here, but the trail you are looking for is to your left, up a small climb. The trail is very narrow here, overgrown with brush, and easy to miss.

Now you cross more rock slabs and then drop down into another shaded grove. Emerging from the last grove, you can see a large rock slab path ahead of you. For the next 0.25 miles, you need to carefully cross the slabs in as straight a line as possible. Look for "ducks" to verify your path. To your right is a large rock face popular with rock climbers. Looking behind you, notice the large rock at the start of this rocky section. Remember this rock to help guide you on your return trip.

When you reach the end of this stretch, you start to hear water flowing nearby. Continue forward and soon you can look down below at a nice section of falls and two deep pools of water along the merged Umpa and Twin Lakes' outlet streams. The trail descends narrowly and at times vaguely, to the water below. The Enchanted Pools are a great place for a break.

To continue to the upper pool, locate the trail above the waterline. This trail parallels the water for another 0.25 miles. The trail dead ends on this side of the creek, and you need to cross through the water to the other side. After crossing, pick up the faint trail to the right. You enter another pine grove and should find the dirt trail easier to follow, zigzagging your way the last 0.25 miles to the lakelet known as "The Enchanted" by locals. Before your arrival, you can easily hear the falls, and can glimpse the water cascading down the rock slabs above the lake. You need to cross its outlet stream to reach its southwest shore. You and your dog will both enjoy this lake and its beautiful waterfalls. Both fishing and swimming are good here.

We have been unsuccessfully trying for years to find the actual Umpa Lake which lies at 7700'. Originally, I thought that the upper pool with its fabulous waterfalls was Umpa, but these pools are at only 7100'. We have followed the output flow up the granite rocks multiple times to only end up at a small pond resplendent with wildflowers and exit to the Twin Lakes Trail as it begins to follow along Twin's outlet stream. Umpa's and Twin's outlet streams converge close to the largest of the Enchanted Pools, so one needs to follow the flows on their left (northeast side) to reach Umpa, rather than from the right (southeast side) and thus reaching Twin.

Upper Enchanted Pool

It is difficult to get to the correct side when the water is flowing heavily, so either attempt this late in the season when crossing is safe, or try mountaineering to this side from off the Tyler Lake Trail. The best spot from that trail would be just after entering Desolation Wilderness and climbing up the first rock gully. From the top of that gully, one can look to the southeast to see the water (or if late in the year, the water stains) on the granite rocks.

Share with: Equestrians and mountain bikers

Notes: Well-intentioned hikers will place the rock "ducks" for you along the trail, however with each season's snowfall the rock piles can fall. Since the forest service does not maintain the trail, the "ducks" are not automatically replaced. You are dependent on the new season's hikers to replace the markers, and not all markers are necessarily accurate.

30 – Meiss Country Trails
El Dorado National Forest

Two trailheads offer access to the Meiss Country in the Carson Pass Area. The first trailhead is just below (west) the Carson Pass Information Center on Highway 88. From the trailhead starting at the Meiss Parking Area, there are two possible hikes.

Directions: Heading east, proceed on Highway 88 17.1 miles past the intersection with Mormon Emigrant Trail to the parking area for the Meiss Trailhead on the left of the highway. Heading west on Highway 88, the parking area is on the right just below the Carson Pass Ranger Station and Information Center.

Meiss Lake

Difficulty: 3
Distance: 4.0 miles to lake
Elevation: Mostly flat, but two climbs in of 250' each and a 300' climb out from lake

Warning: There is no fishing allowed at Meiss Lake since it is a spawning area for the scarce Lahontan cutthroat trout. This is a fee parking area.

Description: This is a pretty hike, mostly flat through scenic meadows on an easy-to-follow trail. The difficulty "3" rating is due to the few difficult climbs along the way. Pay your fee in the envelope at the trailhead ($5.00 in 2016). Start your hike with an easy climb up some boulders. Almost immediately, you start enjoying views of Round Top to the south and Caples Lake below.

This undulating portion of the hike takes you along a hillside, slowly climbing, with switchbacks easing your way up to its top and a pond (about 20 minutes into your hike). After cresting the first ridge, you drop down to Meiss Meadow and cross many streams flowing from the Upper Truckee River. Depending on the previous season's rainfall, these will be either easy rock-hop crossings or some more difficult water jumps. In the first 3.4 miles, you have two climbs, each followed by easy flat stretches across meadows. The Pacific Crest Trail (PCT) shares this portion of the Meiss Meadow Trail. Follow all posts in the direction of Round Lake.

At the end of 3.4 miles, you come to a split in the trail. The PCT continues straight in the direction of Showers Lake. The trail for Meiss Lake heads to the right here and joins the Tahoe Rim Trail (TRT) in the direction of Round Lake and Big Meadow (this marker is at the southern tip of the TRT). At this junction, to the left are a cabin and barn (completed around 1880) remaining from the Meiss (pronounced "mice") family who acquired this land and summered here for many years. A plaque at the site details the family's history (well worth the side trip).

From the junction, you have another 0.6 miles to reach Meiss Lake. The trail passes by the lake, so you need to take a spur trail down to it. As soon as you can view the lake, you will find this spur trail. Pay careful attention to your route down to the lake so you can easily return on the same path. Although fishing is not allowed at Meiss Lake, the shallow waters will provide a warm swimming hole for your lunch break (although we did find leeches in a nearby pond). Be prepared for a strenuous climb out from the lake on your return trip.

More ambitious: Continue a mile beyond Meiss Lake to visit Round Lake (fishing allowed).

Share with: Equestrians (no bikes on the PCT)

Showers Lake
Via Meiss Country Trails

Difficulty: 3

Distance: 5.1 miles to Showers Lake

Elevation: 400' change between high and low points with 200' ascent in first 1.5 miles before descending 400', followed by 360' final ascent

Directions: Follow directions for Meiss Lake parking

Description: For the first 3.4 miles, follow the same trail described for Meiss Lake. At the marker, continue straight on the PCT (also the TRT) in the direction of Showers Lake. For the next mile, you walk through a valley, crossing streams of the Upper Truckee River. Wildflowers dominate the scene, providing many photo opportunities. You descend slightly to a small pond on your right. From here, the trail starts to climb over the next 0.7 miles, gaining 360' to the high point. At this point, notice another trail coming down on your left. This is the trail from Schneider's Cow Camp. You will want to avoid taking this by mistake on your return trip. From here, it is a very short descent to Showers Lake.

Lake water is cold, but you still might enjoy a brief swim. Fishing is fun here, but we caught just small trout and no "keepers." The trail goes around the lake to some nice rocky areas for sunbathing on the far side. If you start to walk around, you will come to a post indicating the continuation of the PCT toward Echo Summit. At this post, there is a spur trail to a lookout point. From here, you can see across the vast wilderness toward Lake Tahoe, and closer below to Dardanelles.

The return hike is pleasant, with enough switchbacks on the last climb to the pond to make it seem almost flat rather than its actual 350' gain. Perhaps the gorgeous view of Round Top (10,381') minimizes the effort. On the final leg, you may enjoy a late afternoon breeze highlighting the quaking aspen lining the trail.

Share with: Equestrians.

Showers Lake
Via Schneider Cow Camp Trail

Difficulty: 3
Distance: 2.1 miles to Showers Lake
Elevation: 370' gain over first 1.2 miles, reaching 9200' at the crest of the trail before descending 550' in the following 0.9 miles to the lake

Directions: Heading east on Highway 88, 14.2 miles beyond the intersection with Mormon Emigrant Trail make a left turn toward the Caples Lake Maintenance Station (0.9 miles beyond the Caples Lake Resort). Heading west on Highway 88, the turn into the Maintenance Station is on the right 3.0 mile west of the Carson Pass Ranger Station and Information Center. Follow the road 0.25 miles to the Maintenance Station and then continue past it onto a graded road. Turn right onto this road and continue 1.65 miles to a gate and a small parking area. The trail begins immediately across from the parking area.

Description: Although a much shorter hike than the one using the Meiss Country Trail, it is still a difficulty '3' due to the elevation gain. The trail starts immediately across from the parking. There is a dirt road to the left, but that is a much longer route to the lake and not advised.

The route starts with just a gradual climb at first, before it intensifies first slightly and then extremely over the opening 1.2 miles. In early July, the wildflower display should be fabulous – one of the best in the area. You emerge from the ascent onto a plateau offering rewarding views worth spending time photographing. From here, take the trail to the left to proceed to the lake. An obscure trail straight ahead would take you down to the Meiss Country Trail after crossing the Upper Truckee River, but the trail is scant and not recommended. A third trail here heads to the right to a couple of peaks. Make a note of this intersection for your return trip.

Continuing on the trail to the left, you have still a short climb before reaching the high point of the hike. You now have a continual 0.8-mile descent down to Showers Lake, with great vistas throughout your journey. Be sure to carry a good map of the area to help you to identify the distant peaks in view, most notably Mt. Rose (10,776'). As you near the lake, take the steeply descending path of loose rocks slowly. At the bottom of the descent, you reach the Pacific Crest Trail (PCT) and make a left turn onto this trail. Make sure to make a note of your exit trail here for when you leave the lake – if you miss this junction (easy to do), you will be back on the Meiss Country Trail and not back in the direction of your vehicle.

The PCT trail portion is a mere 0.1 miles before you reach Showers Lake. Enjoy a relaxing lunch at the lake because a difficult climb faces you for your return hike.

31 – Rockbound Pass Trail
Wrights Lake Recreation Area
Desolation Wilderness

From the Rockbound Pass Trail at Wrights Lake Campground, you have a few options for a day hike. Described here are two possible routes to Maud and to Unnamed Lakes. Later, in the September chapter, the hike to Gertrude and Tyler Lake is described. All of the hikes start at the Rockbound Pass Trailhead.

Maud Lake

Difficulty: 3

Distance: 4.6 miles to lake

Elevation: 640' gain from trailhead to lake, but more vertical feet with first going up, then down to creek, and then back up again making for 1280' actual gain

Directions: From Highway 50 East at Kyburz, continue another 4.8 miles to a left turn onto Wrights Road. Follow this road 8.1 miles into the Wrights Lake Campground. At the Stop sign, continue straight another 0.3 mile to the parking for Rockbound Pass on your left. From the parking area, you cross the street to find the kiosk and day use permits for the Rockbound Trail.

Description: This is a challenging but fun hike with a variety of habitats to explore. Starting from the trailhead, you have a short ascent before a descent to arrive at Beauty Lake in about 15 minutes. At the lake, follow the signs to the Wilderness Area and walk around the lake to your left, ignoring the sign for the Jeep Trail.

Once you leave the lake, follow all posts directing you to Rockbound Trail. Shortly, you will start to enjoy great views of the distant mountain range. Look for the reddish peak and then to its left for the low, saddle area – this is Rockbound Pass. Maud Lake lies below the pass.

Continue to follow the posts in the direction of Rockbound Pass, passing the one for Tyler Lake at 2.1 miles. Shortly after this, you will enter into Desolation Wilderness and a tough ascent of about 0.5 mile. You will arrive at a seasonal pond on your left and then start descending over rock slabs to reach the Jones Fork Silver Creek. This can be a simple "rock hop" crossing, or a very difficult attempt after a heavy rain season. In July of 2006, I had to stop here and turn around, but in June of 2007, I had no problems and was able to continue to Maud Lake.

After crossing the creek, you will ascend over slabs of rocks before reaching Willow Flat. Since it is difficult to follow a trail along rock slabs, conspicuous piles of small rocks have been placed periodically along the way. Look for these rock piles, known as "ducks," to make your way across the slabs.

In Willow Flat, you are welcomed by cooler air, probably a nice breeze, and along with the willows, you have aspens, corn lilies, and ferns. Magnificent rock walls frame the flat, holding in the fresh smell of pines and songs of birds. A small stream nourishes this habitat. You seem to leave it for a climb up and around a large rock, only to return to its shade for a little while longer. When you emerge, a large rock wall ahead confronts you. To your left is a little spur trail, but your trek is up the trail to the top of the rocks.

The 200-foot ascent is difficult, but not too lengthy. Pussypaws and penstemon decorate the rocks. As you near the top, you will pick up the sound of water and can look down to your right to see Silver Creek flowing down a gorge. The trail flattens and you come to the lower part of Maud Lake, which is more like a pond. Continue just a little further to reach the lake itself. If you like to fish, then bring your gear and definitely try your luck.

Less Ambitious Option: Stop at Beauty Lake and enjoy the alpine scenery. This is an easy walk and a nice place to picnic. After a rest, you can continue walking a little further for views of the Crystal Range, and then turn around to return to your car.

Unnamed Lakes

Difficulty: 3
Distance: 4.7 miles to first lake
            0.1 mile to second lake
Elevation: 1020' gain with undulations

Directions: Follow the same directions to the parking and trailhead for Maud Lake.

Description: You will not find the two unnamed lakes you visit on this hike on the map at the trailhead. This will be an unpopular destination on a surprisingly well-marked but unsigned lateral trail. Perhaps because the lakes are shallow and lacking any fish it makes for a seldom-visited spot, but the views are exceptional.

The hike starts on the Rockbound Pass Trail, with Beauty Lake the first stopping point at 0.5 miles. Walk along the lake's shore on the left and start making a short ascent. You climb 440' in 0.3 miles to a post marking your direction for Rockbound Pass to the left. Just fifteen minutes from Beauty Lake, your views open up to distant peaks of the Crystal Range. Look toward the red-colored peak, and then to the left to the low point of the range – this is Rockbound Pass. To the right of the reddish peak, you can see the formation locals refer to as "Dog Rock." See if you can make out the nose, eyes, and ears of the dog.

Continue on the trail another 1.3 miles to your next post. Turn left at the post to continue on the Rockbound Pass Trail. Turning to the right here takes you down to the Loop Trail circling Wrights Lake. This is a good idea for a less ambitious day trip. (You will end up at the main road and need to walk the 0.3 miles to the trailhead parking, but it is a nice beginner's hike.)

In just 0.5 miles, you come to another marker indicating Tyler Lake to the right. You stay straight here on Rockbound Pass. In the next 2.0 miles, you climb into Desolation Wilderness and then descend to the Jones Fork Silver Creek crossing of the merged Maud and Gertrude

Lakes' outlet streams. You may have to venture upstream to find a safe crossing here. After crossing the creek, you continue over rocky slabs before entering into Willow Flat. This is a very peaceful part of the trail, lined with willows and alders. You have a little climb around a rocky section, and then return to the flat. At the end of the flat, you emerge to face a rocky mountain.

The path up the mountain takes you to Maud Lake. Instead, as soon as you emerge from the flat, turn left onto an unmarked dirt trail. Once known as the Cattleman's Lateral Trail, or 16E11, it connects the Rockbound Pass Trail with the Red Peak Stock Trail. Over a pleasant 0.6 miles, you have an easy hike with some great views to the destination lakes. At times, the trail becomes faint and you can get confused. Look up, to your right, whenever you lose sight of the trail and look for the next marker ahead (usually "ducks"). If for any reason you feel unsure of the trail, try going forward a few paces to see if you can see the next marker. If not, then turn around – never risk getting lost. Feel free to place additional markers along the trail for your return trip and for future hikers.

Colors reflect from the shallow water to provide photo opportunities, along with the various colors of the vegetation around the lakes sporting an array of colors. Consider a revisit here in the fall for an exceptional display. Walk to the southwestern shore of the first lake and the second of the two Unnamed Lakes is on your right.

Unnamed Lake #1

You can mountaineer a short distance to the highest rocks for a fantastic view down into Desolation. Turning around from this vantage point, your view is of the Crystal Range. You may be able to hear the sounds from OHVs descending the Barrett Lake Jeep Trail across the canyon. This is a great place to admire the vastness of the wilderness as you enjoy your lunch. If you are looking for a longer hike, continue to the Red Peak Stock Trail.

Share with: Equestrians.

Red Peak Stock Trail

Difficulty: 3

Distance: 6.2 miles additional after leaving the second Unnamed Lake

Elevation: 200' gain to reach the Red Peak Stock Trail, and then the remaining trek has gradual "ups and downs".

Description: Overall, adding this addition to the hike makes for a total of eleven miles, so be sure both you and your pooch are in shape. Additionally, you should not attempt this hike without a map of Desolation Wilderness so you can track exactly where you are at any point. Before leaving the second Unnamed Lake, liberally spray with mosquito repellant. This first trail portion is shaded, with ample streams, and beautiful vegetation. The problem is with the abundant mosquitoes, thousands of them swarming you.

Armed with your map, continue on the main lateral trail another mile beyond the second of the Unnamed Lakes to reach its intersection with the Red Peak Stock Trail. At the junction, two trails take off to the left. The lower one saves you 0.4 miles of hiking. Either one will take you to the Barrett Lake OHV Road. Taking the lower trail, you will reach the jeep road in 0.5 miles. When you reach the jeep trail from the shorter route, you still have 4.7 miles return trip to Dark Lake and then a little further to the wilderness parking.

There are two choices on this return trip, with the one being to go directly to Dark Lake. The other choice takes you off the jeep trail sooner where you can make the short trip over the hill and arrive down at Beauty Lake. You need to look closely for this trail junction to make your way to Beauty Lake. The advantage of using this option is the water opportunity for your dog, and you get off the jeep trail and avoid having to walk along the roadway from Dark Lake back to the parking area. Again, you need a Desolation Wilderness map to understand this route.

32 – Twin Lakes Trail
Desolation Wilderness
Wrights Lake

Difficulty: 3

Distance: 2.7 miles to Lower Twin

3.1 miles to Boomerang and Upper Twin

3.3 miles to Island Lake

Elevation: 1050' gain

Directions: Heading east on Highway 50, continue 4.8 miles past Kyburz to a left turn onto Wrights Road. Travel 8.1 miles to the campground. At the first Stop sign, turn right and go 1.0 mile to the trailhead parking for Twin and Grouse Lakes. If the parking area is full, you will need to return to the Stop sign, turn left, and find the overflow parking area on the left. If you need to park here, then you will add another mile to the hike in both directions. This is a popular trailhead, so get there early for better parking.

Description: You will follow the Twin Lakes Trail to Lower Twin Lake and then continue across its rock dam another 0.4 mile to the more secluded Boomerang Lake. In late July, it should be perfect for swimming, so wear your suit under your hiking clothes. While the hike is not terribly long, it involves a lot of climbing, often in areas exposed to the sun, so remember your hat, sunglasses, and sunscreen.

Starting from the parking area, walk through the service gate and down to the trailhead kiosk. Here you can fill out your day permit for entering Desolation Wilderness. You start on the Loop Trail for an easy 0.4 mile before reaching the Twin Lakes Trailhead on your right signed for Twin, Grouse, Island, and Hemlock Lakes.

From here, you start a 140-foot ascent before reaching a saddle. Then you ascend another 300 feet with Grouse Lake's outlet creek on your left. Within a mile, you will reach the wilderness boundary. Shortly thereafter, you come to a trail post indicating Grouse Lake to the right and Twin Lake to the left. Follow in the direction of Twin Lake.

Soon you will cross the Grouse Lake creek, and depending on the previous rainy season, the crossing is either a simple rock hop or a more difficult challenge. After making the crossing, turn around and make mental notes on where you came across and where the trail is on the other side for your return trip. It is easy to run into difficulties on your return if you do not cross at the same place.

After the creek crossing, you start ascending again over rock slabs. Here you need to look ahead for the next rock piles marking the trail to find your way. These piles of small rocks are "ducks", and they mark many of the trails in Desolation. Over the 1.7 miles from the trail post to Lower Twin Lake, you will be climbing steadily. When you reach the Twin Lake outlet creek, you will hear its waterfall and see it on your left.

At this point, you need to carefully find the trail, which is not the spur taking you over to the creek. Instead, the actual trail bends away from the creek and then ascends more over rocks before bending back toward the creek. Always look ahead for the trail markers made from rock piles. If at any point you are not certain of the trail, then backtrack to the last known marker, and look ahead more diligently for the next marker. Do not advance without being certain of your path. It is a popular trail, so you can always wait for people coming down to see their path, or for someone else coming up the trail so you can follow.

After this last climb, you come to a welcome descent to a little pond. From here, you cross the creek on rock steps and follow the trail up to Lower Twin Lake. When you reach the lake, turn around and make notes as to where the trail ends at the lake. Identify a certain tree or large rock to be your reminder for your return trip; otherwise, it is very difficult to see your exit point.

Lower Twin is the most popular lake along this trail. If it is not busy, then enjoy a moment to relax here and fish. Otherwise, you may want to continue on to the less popular Boomerang Lake, a short 0.4 mile away. To reach Boomerang, cross Twin Lake's rock dam to pick up the trail again. The dam is on your left as you face Twin Lake. (In an extremely heavy rainfall year, the dam may be difficult to cross. If water is flowing over it, then try finding a safer crossing downstream and then come back up from the other side to find the trail again.)

The trail takes you along Twin Lake's western shore and then reaches a rock gully to climb. In a short amount of time, you will reach the smaller Boomerang Lake. Here you can enjoy a pleasant swim and lunch. If it is too crowded, you can opt for Upper Twin Lake directly opposite Boomerang, a short distance from the trail you came from. There is no actual trail down to Upper Twin, but it is easy to make your way down to it to enjoy its seclusion.

Continue 0.2 miles beyond Boomerang Lake to reach Island Lake. This is a popular lake for fly-fishing for trout. From Island Lake, some hikers familiar with the older trails will take off on paths in the direction of Clyde Lake to the east, Mt. Price to the southeast or northwest over to Tyler and Gertrude. These routes require excellent mountaineering skills and detailed maps. I have often spoken with hikers back at the Twin Lakes trailhead parking area who have successfully done these extended routes, but I have never personally tried these off-trail adventures. It is great, however, to see today's hikers continuing to use these old trails.

Less Ambitious Option: Instead of taking the Twin Lake trail, continue on the Loop Trail around the Wrights Lake Recreation Area. This is a peaceful 1.0-mile walk, crossing a bridge from where you can look down to see fish below. Visitors like to kayak or canoe through the waterways that line the trail.

AUGUST

Snow patches are mostly gone now, but the wildflowers still put on a splendid display in the mountains. With a good snow and rain season, you may still find water in the streams, but do not count on it. Carry at least three water bottles, and be sure to have a bowl for your dog. While cooler at the higher elevations, the trails will most likely be dry and dusty now. Hat, sunscreen, sunglasses, and water – all a must for August trails.

Lyons Creek

33 – Carson Pass Trails
Highway 88 Past Caples Lake
Mokelumne Wilderness

You can reach the lakes in the Carson Pass area from two trailheads, with the one from the ranger district office being the more popular. These are heavily used trails due to the great wildflower display annually, but if you venture beyond Winnemucca Lake to Round Top Lake, you will share the trail with fewer hikers.

Winnemucca and Round Top Lakes
Via Woods Lake Trailhead

Difficulty: 3
Distance: 4.6-mile loop
Elevation: 1135' gain from trailhead to Round Top Lake

Directions: Drive east on Highway 88 15.4 miles beyond the intersection with Mormon Emigrant Trail (either take Highway 88 from Jackson, or Highway 50 to Exit 60 in Sly Park to Mormon Emigrant Trail). Find the entrance to Woods Lake Campground on your right just past Caples Lake. Coming west on Highway 88, this entrance is 2.0 miles beyond the Carson Pass Ranger Station. Drive 1.0 mile on its asphalt road to the Woods Lake Trailhead Parking area on your right. There is a day use fee for parking ($5.00 in 2016).

Description: Plan on taking this hike in late July or early August, depending on the severity of the winter. Give the trail time for the snow to melt and the streams to be more easily crossed, yet still enjoy the wildflowers at their peak.

From the parking area, continue on the asphalt road across the bridge to the trail on your right. Continue 0.1 mile to the marked post for Winnemucca Lake to the left and Round Top Lake to the right. Go in the direction to Winnemucca Lake (the other arm is the return route). Cross the asphalt road and find the trail marker on the opposite side.

The first part of the trail is forested and pleasant with just a slight rise. You will cross a stream and enjoy the shaded, well-maintained trail. Notice the blue diamonds in the trees marking the trail for snowshoeing in the winter. After a mile, you will have gained 325' and emerge from your forest shade. Now the views of the distant mountain peaks improve as you hike along the hills of wildflowers, such as mule ears, crimson columbine, waterleaf, showy penstemon, and shooting stars. Shortly, you will enter into the Mokelumne Wilderness. To your right, a spur trail takes you down to a small stream. As you continue ahead the last 0.5 mile to Winnemucca Lake, the climb intensifies, gaining another 440', so take your time and enjoy the views.

Winnemucca Lake is a popular destination, also accessible from the Carson Pass Trailhead. It has beautiful blue, clear water and provides a good fishing spot. As you arrive at the lake, you will notice the post marking the trail up to Round Top Lake. After resting at Winnemucca, continue your hike in the direction of Round Top. This section of the hike is just 1.0 mile, and you will climb another 370'. Looking back down the trail, you have great views of Winnemucca Lake below and ahead Round Top Peak looms. As you arrive at Round Top Lake, look for the post marking the next leg of your loop in the direction of Woods Lake.

Round Top Lake's water is greener and the lake is smaller than Winnemucca. Still, you will find fish here if you want to try your luck. It will be much cooler at this higher elevation (Round Top Peak is 10,381') and most likely windy. Unless it is a very hot day at the start of your hike, expect to be cold at the lake, so take a jacket along in your pack.

From Round Top Lake, take the 2.0-mile trail down to Woods Lake, also called the Lost Cabin Mine Trail. Starting down, you will enjoy great views ahead. Shortly, you can look down to Caples Lake in the distance. The trail follows numerous streams along its descent. In about a mile, you will arrive at remnants of an old mining camp. Leaving the camp, you will continue downhill, picking up views of Woods Lake below. There is a final stream crossing that could be difficult in a heavy rain year, so be safe crossing it.

Notes: Please be respectful of the rules for Mokelumne Wilderness to leash your dog. By following the rules, you ensure the Forest Service will continue to allow dogs into the Wilderness Area in the future.

Winnemucca and Round Top Lakes
Via Carson Pass Trail and Frog Lake

Difficulty: 3

Distance: 2.5 miles to Winnemucca Lake

3.5 miles to Round Top Lake

Elevation: 735' gain from trailhead to Round Top Lake

Directions: Follow the directions for the Woods Lake trailhead parking, but continue east past that location another 2.0 miles to find the parking at the Carson Pass Information Station on your right. There is a parking fee here - $5.00 in 2016.

Description: Unlike the loop trail you hike from the Woods Lake trailhead, this route is "in and out" via Frog Lake. It is the more popular route, most likely due to the start at a higher elevation, saving a 400' gain. The total route, however, is more mileage at 7.0 miles for the total distance in and out compared to the 4.6-mile loop from Woods Lake. At the height of the wildflower season (mid-July), this area is overly crowded on weekends, so waiting until August is a good idea for this trail.

Locate the trailhead starting just beyond the Carson Pass Information Station. This first part of the trail is a part of the Pacific Crest Trail (PCT). You will see its junction on your left, but continue straight in the direction of Frog Lake. You will arrive at Frog Lake shortly after the PCT intersection.

From Frog Lake, you have another 2.0 miles to reach Winnemucca Lake. This is a popular destination in the area, so does not make for a great lunch spot. It is best to continue another mile on to Round Top Lake. Amazingly not very popular, this 1.0-mile section of trail has one of the most magnificent wildflower ecosystems in our area, plus spectacular views in all directions. Round Top Lake is higher and cooler than Winnemucca, so take additional clothing in your pack and cinch down your hand for the windy conditions here.

34 – Lyons Creek Trailhead
Wrights Road
Desolation Wilderness

From the Lyons Creek Trailhead, you have a couple of trail options to explore. If you are looking for an easy day, just plan hiking along the trail portion following the creek and find a nice rock for a snack. By August, the creek's flows will be safer for your dog to enjoy a refreshing dip.

Directions: From Highway 50 heading east, 4.8 miles past Kyburz, turn left onto Wrights Road. Go 4.0 miles to the Lyons Creek Trailhead parking area on your right. There is plenty of parking here, but it is very popular, so if the lot is full continue just a little further to find more parking along the roadside at the creek. At the trailhead, you can find a kiosk with a map and day passes. You need to fill out a pass to enter the wilderness area and deposit the stub in the box at the kiosk.

Lake Sylvia

Difficulty: 4
Distance: 4.6 miles
Elevation: 1320' gain from trailhead to lake

Description: This hike parallels Lyons Creek as you ascend to the lake. The creek, always within earshot, has several access spots for breaks, with sections of falls over larger granite slabs. The first part of the hike goes through meadows of corn lilies and lupine, with other wildflowers mixed in, filling a color palette. While the meadows are beautiful, unfortunately everything that can bite seems to be successful doing so throughout your journey – carry and use your bug spray generously.

After 1.5 miles, you will reach a marker post indicating Bloodsucker Lake (named for its leech inhabitants) to the left. Your destination, Lake Sylvia, is straight ahead. However, a brief 0.1-mile side trip in the direction of Bloodsucker, takes you to a nice spot along the creek for a break before returning to the main trail. At 3.0 miles, you enter Desolation Wilderness and most of the climbing ensues.

At 4.0 miles, you will cross Lyons Creek (if there is too much water, look upstream a short way for an easier crossing). At 4.2 miles, you will come to the marker post for Lyons Lake to the left. Lake Sylvia is straight from here another 0.4 mile. You will cross the Lyons Lake outlet creek and then the outlet from an unnamed lake before reaching Lake Sylvia. All of the creek crossings should be simple rock hops, depending on the previous winter's rain and snowfall. In August, you can swim in Lake Sylvia. Fishing is good here also. For prime viewing of wildflowers, July or early August is best. Take time to walk around the lake for different views. From Lake Sylvia, it is popular to climb up to 9983' Pyramid Peak, so with luck you can sit at lakeside and watch someone else make the effort.

Consider a return trip here in a couple of months to enjoy some beautiful fall colors. Later in the year, it can get cold at the lake, so bring extra layers for fall hikes.

Lyons Lake

Difficulty: 4+
Distance: 4.7 miles to lake
Elevation: 1640' gain

Directions: Follow the same directions to Lake Sylvia for the Lyons Creek Trailhead parking.

Description: This hike to Lyons Lake follows the same first 4.2 miles of the trail to Lake Sylvia. At 4.2 miles, you come to the marker post for Lyons Lake to the left and Lake Sylvia straight ahead. Turn in the direction of Lyons Lake for a steep 0.5-mile climb. At the steepest parts, you may need to use your hands to pull yourself up the rocky slope. Be careful of your footing, and take your time on this difficult portion of the trail.

When you reach the lake, make sure you look backwards and note your entrance route so you can easily start your return when the time comes. If you cross the dam, you will have access to some nice spots around the lake. The lake is high, at 8380', and it can get cold and windy here, so pack extra clothing accordingly. Your trip down should be enjoyable with great views and a pleasant downhill trail.

Tootie Lake
Lyons Creek and Bloodsucker Trails

Difficulty: 2
Distance: 2.3 miles to lake (pond)
Elevation: 640' gain

Directions: Follow directions for Lyons Creek Trailhead parking for Lake Sylvia

Description: This is a nice hike to do when you cannot devote an entire day to the trails. You still break a sweat and get your exercise, and your dog should enjoy all of the water along the way. The wildflowers are striking this time of year, but there will also be a number of biting insects. Carry plenty of insect repellant, and reapply throughout the hike.

Our destination is actually an unnamed lake; however, my dog, Toots, loved splashing in it and we have always referred to it as "Tootie Lake." You need not fill out the day pass at the trailhead, since the hike will not take you into Desolation Wilderness.

Follow the same trail as described for Lake Sylvia for the first 1.5 miles, through the service gate and along the dirt service road, and through the meadows and across the streams. You then come to the post marking the trail for Bloodsucker Lake to the left. This is the direction you want to head, leaving the Lyons Creek Trail for the Bloodsucker Trail. In 0.1 miles, and a 25' descent, you reach the Lyons Creek crossing. At this time of year, this should be a simple rock hop to the other side.

After crossing the creek, the trail winds nicely through a flat for about 0.1 miles before turning left and starting uphill. In the next 0.3 miles, you climb 230' before reaching a little plateau and a slight rest. Then the trail continues uphill another 0.17 miles and another 90' elevation gain. Now you can enjoy a 0.17-mile descent through a pine grove with fern and wildflower undergrowth. You will see the lake (pond) through the trees to your left. Usually ducks will be casually floating on the peaceful water.

Do not be surprised to see a vehicle on the opposite shoreline. There is an Off Highway Vehicle (OHV) road coming from Wrights Road, but only once have I seen a vehicle here. However, I did spot a small black bear on my hike out one time I was there. If you see a bear, stay still and control your dog until the bear leaves. Do not allow your dog to chase or threaten a bear by barking or growling. This is not a popular trail, so enjoy the solitude as you share time with the wildlife.

More Ambitious: You can continue on the trail beyond Tootie Lake and soon reach the post indicating Bloodsucker Lake to the right. This is a short additional 100' climb and 0.5 miles to the lake. The lake, however, is infested with leeches (hence its name), so unless your goal is to visit as many alpine lakes as possible, this might be a good one to skip. If you stay straight instead of turning toward Bloodsucker, you can go another 1.3 miles and end up at the equestrian campground area at Wrights Lake, but your car is four miles back at Lyons Creek.

35 – Big Meadow Trailhead
Lake Tahoe Basin

Two possible routes start at the Big Meadow Trailhead parking area. This is a hub for the Tahoe Rim Trail hikers, so a very busy trailhead.

Directions: Head east on Highway 50 toward Lake Tahoe and then after making the summit, continue another 4.0 miles down to the junction with Highway 89. Turn right onto Highway 89 and go 5.25 miles to the Big Meadow Trailhead parking area on the left. The trail starts at the bottom of the parking area, heading back across Highway 89.

Dardanelles Lake
Tahoe Rim Trail

Difficulty: 3
Distance: 3.5 miles to lake
Elevation: Three climbs in to lake of 250', 535', and 100', and 180' climb out

Description: This is a popular trail, but do not let all the cars deter you. A number of trail users are joggers out for a morning run, so they will be finishing early and leaving the trail open for hikers and mountain bikers. From the parking area, find the trail at the lower end and walk 0.1 mile back to the highway. Carefully cross the highway to find the trailhead for the Big Meadow portion of the Tahoe Rim Trail.

The first part of the trail climbs 250' for 0.4 mile. You will find a fork in the trail at the crest of the hill. The left fork takes you to Scotts Lake. Stay to the right here for Dardanelles Lake and continue into aptly named Big Meadow. The meadow crossing is about 0.2 mile and a pleasant relief after the initial climb.

After enjoying the meadow, the trail starts ascending again through the forest cover. The climb of 535' covers a distance of 1.2 miles and it can be dry and dusty in August. You will be relieved to reach the crest of the hill and ready to start a short descent of 0.2 mile to a trail marker post. If you stay straight, you will continue on to Round Lake. For Dardanelles Lake, take the trail on the right signed Christmas Valley.

Hike 0.2 mile on this leg and find the trail going left across a stream. It may not be marked, so look carefully for the path to the left. Now enjoy the last 1.2 miles of this hike, crossing two more streams and paralleling another for a while. Along the way, cross through a small meadow, site a large Juniper tree along the trail, and absorb the great views. Only at the end, there is a short 100' climb to the lake.

The lake has clear, cool water, probably too cool for a swim, but you can enjoy a little foot soaking or try some fishing for lake trout. A granite cliff lines Dardanelles' south bank. Walk around to the north side and picnic along the flatter granite slabs. Your return hike will be easier with only the 0.2-mile ascent of 180' to confront.

For your return drive, you may want to consider continuing on Highway 89 south to its intersection with Highway 88 in less than 6 miles. Turn right here toward Jackson. This route, although 15 miles longer, will allow you to avoid the busy Lake Tahoe return traffic on Highway 50 and the inevitable backups in Placerville. It also affords a great view into the Kirkwood valley, down to Red Lake and the Carson Pass.

Share with: Equestrians, bikers

Scotts Lake
Toiyabe National Forest

Difficulty: 2
Distance: 2.5 miles to lake
Elevation: 850' gain

Directions: Heading east on Highway 50 toward South Lake Tahoe, you descend from the summit to the valley floor in Meyers. At the bottom of the descent, you will see the sign for Highway 89 South in the direction of Markleeville and Jackson. Turn right onto Highway 89 and drive 5.25 miles to the Big Meadow Trailhead parking area on your left. Park in the lower part of the area, and leave any pull-through spots for horse trailer parking.

Description: This is a very scenic hike, with a steady climb to Scotts Lake. The trail is easy to follow, and nicely shaded. Walk along a meadow, past streams, through large groves of aspen, and enjoy some great views. The wildlife we spotted included a Red-tailed Hawk, grouse, chipmunks, quail, mallards, and a ribbon snake. If following a poor rain season, the lake's waters may be low with a substantial number of exposed tree stumps along the muddy shoreline.

This is a popular trailhead, being a part of the Tahoe Rim Trail system, but Scotts Lake is not a popular destination. Although we had to wait for a parking space to open on our trip over Labor Day Weekend, once we got to the Scotts Lake portion of the hike, we only encountered two pairs of hikers on our way into the lake, and a trio of mountain bikers on the trip out. While at the lake, some quads appeared from the jeep trail that ends at the lake, coming in from another direction. Motorized vehicles are not allowed on the hiking trail itself.

Starting from the lowest end of the parking area, start on the Tahoe Rim Trail (TRT). You immediately need to cross Highway 89 to continue the trail. The first 0.4 miles is a steady 280' climb. When you reach the top of this stretch, you see the post marking the direction to Scotts Lake to your left. (Staying straight here, you would continue on the TRT toward Dardanelles, Round, and Meiss Lakes.) Going left in the direction of Scotts Lake, you will be leaving the Tahoe Rim Trail.

The trail now parallels Big Meadow for a while, offering some nice views. Soon you enjoy the shade of an aspen grove and cross some streams, no doubt still with water. Your hike covers 2.0 miles on a nice dirt footpath, and you can spot willows and alders along the streams, as well as large cedars and rock formations. The wildflowers are spectacular along this trail.

The last 0.1 mile is along a jeep trail. You will immediately see the lake ahead of you. From the jeep trail, make your way down to the water. We tried fishing, but with no success, and never saw any fish jump. Evidence from others who had tried was plentiful, but I cannot attest for anyone's success at Scotts Lake. We did find enough litter to fill a bag, an unfortunate result, no doubt, of the jeep trail that leads to the lake from the opposite direction of the hiking trail allowing for vehicle access to the lake.

Overall, the destination lake on this trail lacks the beauty and solitude of most alpine lakes, but the journey on the trail represents nature's wonders.

Share with: Bikers and equestrians.

36 – Pearl Lake
Barrett Lake Trail
Wrights Lake Recreation Area

Difficulty: 3
Distance: 4.7 miles to lake
Elevation: About 500 feet variation in heights although "ups and downs" make it seem more extreme

Directions: Heading East on Highway 50, you continue 4.8 miles beyond Kyburz and make a left turn onto Wrights Road. Follow Wrights Road 8.1 miles into the campground. At the Stop sign, continue another 0.3 mile to the Rockbound Pass trailhead parking area on the left. The actual trailhead is across the road. You do not need a day permit for hiking to Pearl Lake, as it is not in Desolation Wilderness.

Description: The best part of this hike, in my opinion, is sharing the Jeep portion of the journey with Off Highway Vehicles (OHVs) and watching them maneuver over the rocks and tree roots. The trail is open for OHVs once the ground is dry, while day hikers can go in earlier. If you do not want to share with OHVs then plan on doing this hike earlier in the season when it is only open to hikers.

From the trailhead kiosk, you start on the Rockbound Pass trail and hike 0.5 mile to Beauty Lake. From the lake, you will see a trail marker indicating the Jeep Trail to your left. You walk about 800 feet on this trail before intersecting with the Barrett Lake Trail. Head to your right on the jeep trail, making a note for your return trip of this side trail back to Beauty Lake (if you miss it on your return, you will just continue on the road trail to Dark Lake and then to the parking area for Rockbound Pass).

Once on the jeep trail, you will see immediately a small pond on your left. You will follow the jeep trail slowly downhill until reaching a creek crossing for Jones Fork Silver Creek. By September, this crossing should be easy enough, but if there is still too much water, look upstream at some large boulders to help you safely across.

After crossing the creek, you will start an ascent with the creek following down below the trail on your right. The trail eventually leaves the creek and continues ascending. When you finally reach the top, you reach a flat area called Mortimer Flat. From this flat, look along the main trail to your left for a side trail that takes us to Pearl Lake. (The last time I hiked this, the side trail was marked with three blue ribbons on trees.) From the trailhead to this side trail, you will have gone about 2.6 miles.

Leaving the Jeep Trail behind, this next part of the trail is quiet and very pretty, with pines to shade and meadows of wildflowers. You will enjoy a little downhill meandering before starting another ascent. When you reach the top of this hill, you can look down to a private lake below. The trail then starts downhill, arriving at the fence line for the private land.

Shortly after reaching the fence line, there is a spur trail on your right marked with rock piles. This spur will take you to the main trail to Pearl Lake. If you miss the spur, just continue along the fence line and arrive at the private house. Here you will easily see the Pearl Lake sign pointing you to the main trail for the 0.5-mile hike into the lake.

Pearl Lake does not get many hikers, so it is a peaceful lunch spot. Do not forget to bring your camera so you can photograph this pretty, alpine lake with its lilies, rock dam, and awesome reflections from the surrounding trees. On your trek back, you can take time to enjoy the distant peaks of the Crystal Range.

Share with: OHVs

37 – Echo Lakes Trail
El Dorado National Forest

Numerous hikes are available from the Echo Lakes trailhead, many sharing the PCT.

Directions: Heading east on Highway 50, drive 6.0 miles beyond Twin Bridges and make a left onto Johnson Pass Road. Drive 0.5 mile to a left onto Echo Lakes Road. Continue 1.0 mile down Echo Lakes Road to the large parking area above the resort. There are both paved and dirt parking areas. A trail down to the resort starts from the dirt parking lot, signed on a tree. You walk steeply down the trail (100' descent in 0.15 mile) to reach the resort. Do not be concerned that all of the cars in the lot represent hikers. This is where all of the cabin owners and their guests also park. Nevertheless, it is a very popular trail.

While a busy trail, there are so many lakes to visit in the area, the hiker population divides nicely amongst them, and you are likely to find the seclusion you are seeking in the wilderness. When you walk down to the resort, look for the boat chalet down by the water. Here you can pay for your passage on the water taxi. Prices in 2016 were $14.00 one way per person and $5.00 per dog. This is an August hike, and it will likely be hot, so seriously consider treating yourself to the boat ride and shorten your hike by 2.5 miles in each direction. Call ahead to (530) 659-7207 to verify taxi times, days of operation, and prices. Usually the taxi stops running after Labor Day Weekend and it will not run without at least three paying riders. The Desolation Wilderness kiosk with Day Use Permits is across from the boat chalet.

Lake Margery and Lake Lucille

Difficulty: 3

Distance: 3.0 miles to Lake Margery

              3.1 miles to Lake Lucille

              (Add 2.5 miles if you do not take the water taxi)

Elevation: 840' ascent from boat trail to highest point

Description: If you are not taking the taxi, cross the metal bridge at the lake's dam, and make a short uphill climb to reach the trail. The trail will follow along Lower and Upper Echo Lake, with views down to the water and the cabins dotting its shoreline. It is a mostly flat 2.5 miles, with only a 20' overall elevation gain before you intersect with the trail coming up from the dock where the water taxi drops off hikers.

If you take the water taxi, verify the latest time for a return ride that day. Be sure to return to the dock well before that time. You will see a small wood building near the pier at the drop off point. The telephone to call the taxi is in the building. From the pier, climb uphill shortly to reach the PCT. Make a mental picture of this spot so you can find it on your return.

From the point where the dock trail reaches the PCT, head west (to the left) and climb 0.6 miles and 280' before reaching the wilderness boundary. The first part of the trail from the boat dock to the wilderness boundary is rocky and exposed to the sun. Bring a sun hat and use sunscreen. You may start to doubt the hike's recommendation during the first 20 minutes of the journey. Be patient, the trail and conditions will improve, and the destination lake will be well worth your efforts. Take caution with your footing on the loose rocks. Once you enter the wilderness, you will get patches of shade and fewer rocks to maneuver.

As soon as you enter the wilderness, you start to see posts directing you to the various lakes along the trail. Stay on the PCT in the direction of Lake Aloha. The first post directs you to Triangle Lake on your right. Continue on the PCT another 0.5 miles and find a post on your left directing you to Tamarack Lake (a worthy side trip). Do not leave the PCT. Continue another 0.6 miles to the next post on your right pointing you to another trail for Triangle Lake. Just shy of this post for Triangle Lake, the PCT will have made a sharp turn uphill to the right, and then a couple of switchbacks on the way up to the Triangle Lake post.

Echo Lakes Trail

Continue on the PCT past this second post signed for Triangle Lake. You are now going to enjoy this next 1.0-mile of trail with its flatter, shadier trek through impressive Haypress Meadow. In August, the wildflowers will be sparser, but still enjoyable. Along this one-mile stretch, you pass numerous trail posts for other lakes, first for Lake of the Woods, and then one for Lake Lucille. Do not take this first post's trail to Lake Lucille. There will be another post for Lake Lucille and another trail that you take into the lake. On your return trip, you will make a small loop and come out on this earlier trail to return to the PCT.

After the first post to Lake Lucille, continue another 0.4 miles, with a view down to Lake Margery, and then see a post on your left directing you to Lake Aloha. Here you stop following in the direction of Lake Aloha. Veer right instead and stay on the PCT for a very short distance to a post marking your way to Lake Lucille. Take this right arm of the trail. You first come to Lake Margery in about one-third of a mile. From Lake Margery, the trail continues around the north side of the lake and down to Lake Lucille.

When you see Lake Lucille, stay on the trail closest to the water. This trail goes along the lake's west shoreline to its northern end. Definitely follow along to the that end of the lake and then just beyond a short distance on a spur trail for an awesome view down to Fallen Leaf Lake, Lake Tahoe, and the casinos in the distance. Enjoy your stay at beautiful, serene Lake Lucille. Try fishing here for trout (Jeff had a 16-inch one bite his hook), or just swim, relax, and watch the ducks splashing and dunking as they look for food.

When you are ready to leave the lake, take the trail back to the southwest end of the lake. You should see another trail to your left (not the one you came in on). This trail takes you uphill about 200' elevation gain back to the PCT. Retrace your steps back to the pier.

More Ambitious Option: On the return hike, once on the PCT, in about 0.1 miles you will see the post again for Lake of the Woods. Consider a 0.7-mile side trip to visit this much larger lake.

Triangle Lake

Difficulty: 3
Distance: 2.9 miles to lake, 1.6 miles on a return loop
Elevation: 720' gain

Directions: Same trailhead as for Lake Margery and Lake Lucille

Description: As an alternative to visiting Lake Lucille, you can visit Triangle Lake for a shorter outing. Follow the trail guide for Lake Lucille until you reach the second post directing you to Triangle Lake.

You will be returning on a loop to the PCT and emerge at the earlier post.

Once you leave the PCT, you have a very pleasant downhill hike, dropping 60' over the next 0.8 miles. During this stretch, you have nice views down to Tamarack and Ralston Lakes, as well as across to Ralston Peak (9235'). At the bottom of this portion of trail, you reach a junction with the first trail to the lake. Head north here (left at the junction) and in just 0.4 miles, you will reach Triangle Lake, dropping 160' to the lake.

Triangle is a fun lake to visit, as you are able to walk around its shoreline, trying out various fishing spots. This is not a popular destination lake, so you may find it all to yourself. On your return hike, after you ascend the 160' back to the trail junction, you can choose to stay straight on the trail for a shorter hike back to the PCT and to the pier.

September

38. Gerle Creek
39. Glen Alpine Trails
40. Penner Lake
41. Silver Lake Trails
42. Granite and Grouse Lakes (Mokelumne Wilderness)
43. Gertrude and Tyler Lake

September is a great time to continue your hiking year, with mosquitoes abated, cooler temperatures, and crowds diminished. Colors are starting to change in the foliage, and crossing creeks is easier, inspiring you to continue to hit the trail.

Grass Lake

38 – Gerle Creek
Crystal Basin Recreation Area
Ice House Road

Difficulty: 1
Distance: 0.5-0.7 mile one-way
Elevation: This is a flat trail, with only a 10' elevation change

Directions: From Highway 50 going east, turn left onto Ice House Road immediately after crossing the bridge over the South Fork American River (about 22 miles east of Placerville). Follow Ice House Road 26.5 miles to a left turn into Gerle Creek (this will be 2.8 miles beyond the right turn for Loon Lake). Drive 1.0 mile into the campground and through the campsites to reach the day use parking area (no fee for the day use area).

Description: Gerle Creek offers one of the best interpretive trails in this area. Take the time to read all of the markers, as they are full of interesting information. The flat trail is not only good for those with physical limitations, but also fun for children with its interpretive signs explaining how the Indians used nature's bounty for their food, shelter, clothing, and medicines.

From the parking area, locate the sign for the Lake Shore Trail. This trail goes 0.7 mile to the dam. For most of the distance (0.5 mile), the Lake Shore Trail joins with the Summer Harvest Trail. The Summer Harvest Trail is an interpretive trail with 14 markers describing each scene and the ways the Indians used nature for making their food, medicines, homes, clothes, and trade items. The markers give you complete descriptions of the scenes, and suggest points for you to smell a tree, or touch a grinding rock. The trail is wheelchair accessible, flat, and shaded. Benches are available along the shoreline.

The Summer Harvest Trail ends at the last post comparing life then and now. You can continue the final way to the dam on a lesser path (not suitable for disabled travelers).

The dam works to form a peaceful lake out of Gerle Creek. Enjoy your stay at the reservoir, picnic, or fish for brown trout. Motorboats are not allowed on this lake, making for an idyllic site for canoeing.

39 – Glen Alpine Trails
Desolation Wilderness

The Glen Alpine trailhead offers a number of different hike options, with varying lengths and difficulty levels. This is an extremely popular trailhead, but now in September you will be more likely to find an available parking spot.

Directions: At the "Y" in South Lake Tahoe, continue straight on Highway 89 in the direction of Tahoe City. Drive 3.1 miles, just past Camp Richardson, and turn left onto Fallen Leaf Road. Continue for 4.9 miles to a junction with Road 12N15 (to the right).

Stay straight here on Fallen Leaf Road (Road 12N16) another 0.4 miles to reach the parking area for the Glen Alpine Trail. This is a popular hike, but less crowded in September. Still, you may need to park along the roadway if the paved parking area is full.

Mt. Tallac via Gilmore Lake

Difficulty: 5
Distance: 4.3 miles to Gilmore Lake
6.1 miles to Mt. Tallac
Elevation: 1760' gain to Gilmore Lake
3195' to Mt. Tallac at 9735'

Directions: Start at the Glen Alpine Trailhead described above
Description: This is a long hike with a lot of elevation gain, so plan on making this a long, strenuous, day's journey. You will definitely want to

have the time to rest at Gilmore Lake before making the final 1.8-mile ascent of 1435' to Mt. Tallac. Start your day early to assure returning to your car before dusk.

Lily Lake is the body of water you can see from the parking area. An inviting meadow surrounds the lake, beckoning you to explore, but with Mt. Tallac in your future, there is no time to waste. Starting from the parking area, walk along the gated service road for 1.1 miles and climb 440', before starting on the actual Glen Alpine Trail. This is mostly loose, small rocks, so consider your dog's feet before starting out. You do pass by a nice waterfall on this part of the trail, which parallels Glen Alpine Creek. Signage on this part of the trail indicates both Grass and Susie Lakes ahead.

You arrive at historic Glen Alpine Spring, discovered by Nathan Gilmore (Gilmore Lake's namesake) in 1863. Here you can find an informational kiosk giving you the history of the Glen Alpine area. Shortly from the spring, the actual foot trail begins. In 0.5 miles, you reach a trail junction, indicating Grass Lake to the left, and Susie Lake and Mt. Tallac straight ahead.

Continue straight in the direction of Mt. Tallac, entering Desolation Wilderness, and climbing another 820' over the next 1.6 miles to the next trail junction. This is a very steep climb, with sections of sun exposure. Fortunately, there are several access spots to streams along the way as the trail parallels Gilmore Lake's outlet stream.

From the trail marker, you can go left to Susie Lake (see Trail #35 (B)) in the direction of Lake Aloha, or continue in the direction of Half Moon Lake, Gilmore Lake, and Mt. Tallac. Continue straight here and follow signs in the direction of Gilmore Lake. In a short 0.3 miles, you reach another junction, and again stay the course in the direction of Gilmore Lake.

From this junction, you are now on part of the PCT. Follow the PCT for just 0.6 miles, and climb another 400' before reaching another junction on the trail. Turn right in the direction of Gilmore Lake, just a short 0.1 miles from here.

Be sure to rest at Gilmore Lake before starting the last leg of your trek to Mt. Tallac's peak. You will climb 1200' over the next 1.6 miles before reaching the last trail junction. A trail coming in from your left is the one coming from the Mt. Tallac Trail that takes you past Floating Island and Cathedral Lakes (the original route described in *48 Dog-Friendly Trails*). Stay straight here, and in just 0.2 miles, you reach the peak, climbing a final 235'.

The views from Mt. Tallac, at 9735', are spectacular, with many alpine lakes in sight. Be sure to have a good map of Desolation Wilderness with you so you can identify the lakes and peaks decorating the scene.

Susie Lake

Difficulty:	3
Distance:	4.3 miles to Susie Lake
	5.2 miles to Heather Lake
	6.1 miles to Lake Aloha
Elevation:	1160' gain to Susie Lake

Directions: Start at the Glen Alpine Trailhead described above

Description: Follow the trail directions for the hike to Gilmore Lake and Mt. Tallac for the first 3.3 miles when you reach a trail post directing you to Lake Aloha to the left and Gilmore Lake straight. Take the trail to the left to reach Susie Lake.

This next portion of the trail is a very pleasant stretch after the strenuous climb you just finished. You drop about 100' over the next 0.5 miles, and you pass by a number of ponds (some may be dry now in September). You may need some insect repellant for this stretch of the trail.

You reach another trail junction, with Gilmore Lake to the right and Lake Aloha to the left. Travel in the direction of Lake Aloha, now on the PCT, and reach Susie Lake in another 0.5 miles. Susie Lake is a very pretty lake, featuring a small island, and with good beach access.

We enjoyed a brisk swim here, with minnows bumping against our legs. This is a great lake for your lunch break before returning to your vehicle.

More Ambitious: Continue from Susie Lake to Heather Lake, just 0.9 miles away. You cross Susie Lake's outlet stream (be sure to visit its waterfall a little downstream), and then have a leisurely walk along this portion of the PCT. Heather Lake has good fishing. From here, it is just another 0.9 miles to Lake Aloha.

Grass Lake

Difficulty: 2
Distance: 2.6 miles
Elevation: 700' gain

Directions: Start at the Glen Alpine Trailhead described above

Description: Start this hike following the described route for Mt. Tallac and Susie Lake. Doing this shorter trail, you will have time to better enjoy Lily Lake and explore the Glen Alpine Resort area. From the spring, if you walk toward the sounds of water you can find a couple of nice pools.

From the Glen Alpine Spring area, take the dirt trail and reach a trail junction in 0.5 miles. Go left in the direction of Grass Lake. You now enter into Desolation Wilderness and cross Gilmore Lake's outlet stream. In 0.2 miles, you reach a grassy pond (not Grass Lake) formed from Glen Alpine Creek. This is a pleasant spot with distant views of peaks. Cross the pond to continue on the dirt trail, visible on the other side. You can use a combination of downed logs and rocks to cross straight over to the visible trail.

You now have just 0.7 miles and a short ascent of about 200', broken up with numerous switchbacks, before reaching Grass Lake. The trail continues 0.2 miles along its western shore to a landing between two arms of the lake. The day we visited the lake, it was extremely windy and too cool for a swim, but on a calmer day, you could enjoy its warm, shallow waters. It was also too cool to try fishing, but generally, the more shallow lakes have poorer fishing.

40 – Penner Lake
Grouse Lakes Area
Tahoe National Forest

Difficulty: 2
Distance: 0.1 mile to Carr Lake
                  0.3 miles to Feeley Lake
                  1.7 miles to Island Lake
                  3.2 miles to Penner Lake
Elevation: 225' gain

Warning: 2.8 miles driving on rough, dirt road

Directions: About 40.0 miles east of Auburn on I-80, take Exit 161 for Highway 20 West. Continue on Highway 20 in the direction of Nevada City for 4.2 miles and turn right onto Bowman Lake Road (Road 18). Drive 8.5 miles on Bowman Lake Road, crossing South Fork Yuba River and passing by Fuller Lake. Turn right at the sign for Lindsey, Feeley, and Carr Lakes (Road 17). The road now becomes a mixture of dirt and rocks, but not extremely rutted. Continue 2.1 miles and then follow the sign to Carr Lake, veering to the right. It is just another 0.7 miles now to the parking area for the trailhead. Do not block the service gate.

Description: This is a lovely hike, and one that the whole family should enjoy. Starting at the service gate, walk along the service road to the information kiosk with the trail map. Continue on the road and immediately you see Carr Lake on your right. Just above Carr Lake, you find a restroom and a great vista point down to the lake. To your left, you see the dam for Feeley Lake above you on the trail. Walk up to the dam, and find the start for Round Lake Trail. You will have climbed about 60' in this first 0.3-mile section.

Round Lake Trail goes along the shores of Feeley Lake for 0.7 miles before heading away, uphill. As you leave Feeley Lake, the trail splits, but both trails merge in a short distance. The uphill climb of 0.2 miles gains about 150' before dropping down to petite Delaney Lake (resembling more a pond). The trail goes to the left at the lake and then follows along its northern edge. In 0.4 miles, you reach the junction with Crooked Lakes Trail. Here you leave Round Lake Trail, and go left onto Crooked Lakes Trail. On a future trip, you can continue on Round Lake Trail and visit the lakes it traverses – Long, Round, and Milk Lakes.

Feeley Lake in May

In 0.1 miles, the Crooked Lakes Trail arrives at two lakes and takes you between them, one a small, unnamed lake and the other a larger, appropriately named Island Lake. A summer trip here would invite you to swim to the islands for a pleasant dip, but now the waters are chilly, "but you get used to it" swore some teenage girls. The trail continues 0.75 miles along the lake's western shore to its northern end. Avoid any spurs taking you away from the lake during this stretch of the trail

Continuing beyond Island Lake, in the next 0.5 miles you first pass by a large pond before arriving at a smaller one. From this second pond, you can see Penner Lake to your right. For the best access to Penner Lake, skip the spur at the pond taking you down to the eastern shore, and instead stay on Crooked Lakes Trail a little longer beyond the pond. The trail takes you through a cool, garden setting and then up a rocky hill. When you get above the pond and can look down to the lake, you see another spur trail to take you to its north-west side. Taking this route, you reach Penner Lake in 0.25 miles to find a very scenic spot sporting some good fishing opportunities. On this side of the lake, you have good rock drop-offs into deep water for fishing.

The entire Grouse Lakes Area is dotted with alpine lakes, so acquire a Tahoe National Forest map for the Sierra Buttes/Donner Pass area at the Nevada City Ranger Station (530-265-4531) or your local REI. Study the map and plan an enjoyable outing on any of the many trails in the area.

Share with: Bikers and equestrians. (While there was evidence of horses on the trail, pulling a trailer on the dirt road to the trailhead is not advisable, so for horses park just off Bowman Road and ride in on the dirt road.)

More ambitious: Beyond Penner Lake on the Crooked Lakes Trail, you could continue up the ridge and then down to Upper Rock Lake, but this trail portion is non-maintained. (For another trail to the Rock Lakes on a future visit, follow the dirt road in the direction of the Lindsey Lakes Trail and enjoy a maintained trail visiting Lindsey, Culbertson, and Rock Lakes.)

41 – Silver Lake Trails
Granite and Hidden Lakes
El Dorado National Forest

Difficulty: 2

Distance: 1.5 miles to Lower Granite Lake

                   1.6 miles to Upper Granite Lake

                   3.6 miles to Hidden Lake

Elevation: 230' gain to Granite Lake

                   375' gain to Hidden Lake

Directions: Coming from Placerville, you can travel on Highway 50 east to Exit 60 for Sly Park and follow Sly Park Road around the lake to a left turn onto Mormon Emigrant Trail, and then drive 25 miles to the junction with Highway 88. If coming from the Jackson area, you can travel on Highway 88 in the direction of South Lake Tahoe.

From the junction of Mormon Emigrant Trail onto Highway 88, you now drive east for 6.9 miles to Silver Lake and turn south in the direction of Kit Carson Lodge. Driving west on Highway 88, this entrance is 10.4 miles beyond the Carson Pass Ranger Station.

In 0.1 miles, follow the sign directing you toward Kit Carson Lodge. In another 0.3 miles, the turn for the lodge goes to the right, but you stay straight here and continue along the narrow road through the campground area and along Silver Lake. In 0.5 miles, the road forks, with the right fork taking you to some cabins. Take the left fork here and continue another 0.3 miles to a right turn in the direction of "Granite Lk." In just a short 0.1 miles, there is another right turn in the direction of "Campfire Girls." You reach the parking area for Granite Lake at the end of the road in 0.2 miles. If the area is full for this popular hike, then park along the roadside safely off the road.

Description: This is a nice family-friendly adventure. Your trail starts below the parking area at a sign marked for "Minkalo Trail 17E72", "Granite Lake 1", and "Plasse 3" (mileages are rounded down to an even number on the sign). This is a very easy to follow dirt trail, with only minor rocks to pass across. You can easily pick up the footpath as you look across the rock slabs. In July, water should be plentiful along the trail for your dog – but always carry doggy water just in case. Also, plan to come across a number of horses, since this is a very popular equestrian trail.

The trail immediately starts an easy ascent of 90', with views to the north of the south side of Thunder Mountain (see Trail #34). The trail passes a small pond (dry in August), and after 0.5 miles reaches a bridge crossing Squaw Creek. Your ascent continues with another 100' gain, reaching a plateau with a view down to Silver Lake. At about 1.0 miles on the trail, you reach a post directing you to Allen Camp (3 miles to the right on 17E72), or to Granite Lake (0.5 miles ahead on 17E23). Continue here in the direction of Granite Lake.

Granite Lake has two bodies of water, and you reach the lower one first at 1.5 miles. Continuing another 0.1 miles on the trail, you reach the upper lake at 1.6 miles. The upper body of water is the one actually named Granite Lake. Locals told us there were leeches in the water, but we did not see any, and Toots was fine with going into the lake. Nevertheless, you might want to avoid the urge to swim on this outing.

The only difficult trail reading on this hike is at upper Granite Lake, appropriately named for the granite slabs around it. You may have a problem seeing the dirt path ahead, but the trail goes around the southwest end of the lake and you can pick up the path again at the other end of the lake. Turn around here and get a visual picture of the trail for your return trip.

The trail now flattens and continues south in the direction of Hidden Lake. You pass by two ponds, and walk through a nice meadow of wildflowers. A mile after leaving Granite Lake, and a mere 40' climb, you will find a sign indicating you have another mile to Hidden Lake.

Now the trail climbs another 100', and you pass over some rocky stretches. You cross an outlet stream from Silver Lake (a tiny puddle by August) and then climb a short distance before getting your first peek at Hidden Lake. Before walking down to the lake's shoreline, visually note your trail for the return trip; otherwise, you will find it difficult to pick up the trail in the lake's rocky approach.

Hidden Lake is a shallow lake, with ducks and lots of water insects, but no fish that we could see. It is a nice spot for having your lunch before your return trip.

Share with: Joggers, bikers, and equestrians. This trail is very popular with equestrians, and there are numerous spur horse trails along the main trail to confuse you at times. The described parking area is not for horse trailers. If you trailer a horse, then turn instead into Plasse's Resort (the turn west of Kit Carson Lodge) to find parking suitable to trailers. You can then ride up the Allen Camp Trail to reach the Granite Lake Trail system.

42 – Granite and Grouse Lakes
Mokelumne Wilderness
Blue Lakes

Difficulty: 5 to Grouse Lake (2 to Granite Lake)
Distance: 2 miles to Granite Lake
6 miles to Grouse Lake
Elevation: 540' gain to Granite Lake
600' gain from Granite to high point on trail (undulating trail nets you a lot more feet climbed)

Directions: From Highway 50 in Pollock Pines, take Exit 60 for Sly Park Road. As you exit the freeway, take a right onto Sly Park Road and continue 4.6 miles around Jenkinson Lake. Make a left onto Mormon Emigrant Trail and go about 25 miles to its end at Highway 88. Make a left and head east on Highway 88 for 23.7 miles and turn right onto Blue Lakes Road. Continue on Blue Lakes Road for 11.6 miles to reach the park entrance. Turn right, in the direction of Lower Blue Lake. The first 0.2 miles are a paved surface; and then 1.4 miles on unpaved road takes you to just past Middle Creek campground and the crossing over Middle Creek. Locate the parking for the Grouse Lake Trailhead on the left.

Description: This is a long hike, and for the most part (except the last 1.5 miles on the return trip) it seems mostly uphill in both directions, due to the undulating course. You will gain over 1100' in the first 5.5 miles before dropping 400' down to Grouse Lake. Give yourself plenty of time for this hike so you can rest at the lake before starting the 400' ascent out of its bowl. Pack along a good map of the Mokelumne Wilderness to help you identify landmarks.

From the parking area, walk down toward Upper Blue Lake and cross the metal bridge over the spillway. After crossing the bridge, you see the trail sign on your left for trail 18E08. The trail starts paralleling the road, and soon you need to cross on a log over Middle Creek. After crossing, continue on this parallel path and avoid a couple smaller spur trails. Remember this log crossing on your return, as it is easy to miss and you could end up on one of the spurs instead of returning to the parking area.

The first mile is shaded and gradual and then you reach the Mokelumne Wilderness border sign. From here, you continue to climb, shortly reaching a nice pond. At the pond, the trail goes around to the left to reach the other side. You reach picturesque Granite Lake at 2.0 miles. Granite Lake is the larger of the two lakes on this trail. There is good fishing here for cutthroat trout.

If your goal is to continue to Grouse Lake, follow the trail along the left, southern shore of Granite Lake. For the next 3.5 miles, you continually ascend 600' and then drop down to spring crossings. The summits for each ascent hover around 8800', close to a problem area for those who may suffer from symptoms of **altitude sickness**. The trail is mostly a dirt footpath, and poorly marked in some places. Generally, you can look off in the distance to pick up the footpath again. The views on this difficult stretch are stunning, with distant peaks, including The Nipple, and sights of lakes below you.

Finally, at the last summit, you get your first glimpse down to Grouse Lake. Fishing is also good at Grouse Lake if you want to take the time to try it. When rested, start your return trip. You should plan on at least three hours of hiking in each direction for this journey. Also, remember to watch for the log crossing at the end of the hike.

Did you know? Altitude sickness can hit anyone, starting at 8000' elevation and above (for me, about 8800'). The air at higher altitudes being "thin" on oxygen causes it. Symptoms can vary and are likened to the flu or a hangover (for me, symptoms include fatigue, dizziness, and nausea). It can also cause a headache, sometimes quite severe. Your fingernails can turn purple from the lack of oxygen as well.

If you start experiencing any of these symptoms while hiking at high altitudes, stop immediately and take a break. Give your body time to adjust to the new altitude. Open your lungs by spreading your arms out away from your body and breathing deeply. Although you may not feel like eating, do drink a quantity of water. Once the symptoms disappear, you can advance to a higher elevation. Be sure you are OK before continuing, because the sickness can also affect your brain, causing confusion, faintness, and clumsy walking – all dangerous conditions for hiking. If you cannot ease the symptoms, do not continue to higher elevations. Avoid possible injury and head carefully to a lower elevation. Never let anyone with altitude sickness symptoms leave the group to go to a lower elevation alone.

43 – Gertrude and Tyler Lake
Rockbound Pass Trail
Wrights Lake Recreation Area

Difficulty: 4
Distance: 4.2 miles to Gertrude
Elevation: 1040' to Gertrude

Directions: From Highway 50 East at Kyburz, continue another 4.8 miles to a left turn onto Wrights Road. Follow this road 8.1 miles into the Wrights Lake Campground. At the Stop sign, continue straight another 0.3 mile to the parking for Rockbound Pass on your left. From the parking area, you cross the road to find the kiosk and day-use permits for the Rockbound Trail.

Description: Return to the Rockbound Pass Trail late in the summer for this more difficult hike to Gertrude and Tyler Lake. For the first 2.0 miles, the climb is a moderate 300' making for a good warm-up for the second half of the hike. Follow all signs for Rockbound Pass until you reach the post pointing to Tyler Lake to your right (about one hour of hiking). Turn here to leave the Rockbound Pass Trail and start on Tyler Lake Trail. The trail briefly passes through a flat with alders before starting its climb to the Desolation Wilderness boundary.

Avoid all spurs taking you to the right, instead heading straight until you reach the boundary sign. At the sign look for the trail on your right and start your ascent. This is the first of three gullies to climb on this hike. Avoid spurs to the right and look ahead for rock piles known as "ducks" to guide your way. This first gully is about a 200' ascent. At the top, you can look down to your right to Umpa Lake and Wrights Lake in the distance.

From here, the trail heads briefly down hill to your left. Then you start the 140' climb up the second gully. At the top, you have a pleasant, but short, walk through a forested saddle before arriving at the final gully. This third gully is a 75' ascent and again tops out at a flat, forested area. You then reach another rocky climb of about 235' over rocky slabs; the trail is faint in spots before you reach a pond on your left (could be dry by now).

The pond area is pleasant, forested with hemlocks, the trail following the natural runoffs from spring. By this time of year, the trail will be dry and easier to follow. Enjoy this section for its short span and then prepare for another rocky climb. The trail can be difficult to follow, so make sure you clearly see your path or the next "ducks" marking your way before proceeding forward. You then cross over the Tyler Lake outlet stream, most likely dry now in September. This crossing can be quite difficult earlier in the season. Soon now, you will arrive at shallow Gertrude Lake.

You have two possible side trips on your return hike. When you reach the outlet stream from Tyler Lake, you can follow it uphill a short distance to reach the lake itself. This is an unmarked path, and a little brushy in sections, but overall an easy mountaineering to an alpine lake in just 0.1 miles. At Tyler Lake, you should definitely find some solitude. Originally, the Tyler Lake trail actually led you to this lake rather than to Gertrude Lake. Over the years, the trail has changed course, but the name remains.

If you are not comfortable with mountaineering, instead try a short excursion in the other direction from Tyler Lake. When you start your return trip, after 0.25 mile, look on your right for willow bushes and a spur trail taking you to Tyler's grave with its white marble headstone. Tyler, a ranch hand, died in a snowstorm in 1882 and this beautiful setting honors him with a final resting spot.

Enjoy the rest of the hike back to your car, now mostly downhill. Great viewing spots abound on your trip out. The wildflowers are long gone now, replaced with the beginnings of autumn brown and gold grasses. In another month, more fall colors will be on display.

October

44. Ralston Peak and Cup Lake
45. Tallac Historic Site and Taylor Creek Visitor Center
46. Mt. Tallac via Floating Island Lake
47. Lake Margaret
48. Round and Bryan Meadows

The days are cooler, so it is a great time to try some more difficult hikes, like the ones to Ralston Peak and Mt. Tallac. October is also a great month to view some great fall colors, especially predominate on the hikes to Lake Margaret and Round and Bryan Meadows. The visit to Camp Richardson and the Tallac Historic Site and Taylor Creek Visitor Center is timed to catch the annual Kokanee run. It is always a great time to visit dog-friendly Kiva Beach for your pooch to enjoy a swim in Lake Tahoe.

Trail sign for Bryan and Round Meadows

44 – Ralston Peak and Cup Lake
Mt. Ralston Trail
Camp Sacramento

Difficulty: 5
Distance: 4.1 miles to the peak via Option #1
Elevation: 2715' gain

Directions: Heading east on Highway 50, a mile past Twin Bridges there is a passing lane. You will see Sayles Flat and Camp Sacramento on the right. Alongside the passing lane, there is a center turn lane for the Mt. Ralston Trail parking area. This area is directly across from Camp Sacramento.

From the parking area, you will see a dirt jeep road. You can drive up this road to a smaller parking area at the trailhead, or park down below at the highway turnout. Parking at the trailhead will save you a little effort. At the trailhead, you can find day use permits to fill out for entry into Desolation Wilderness. Mileages and elevations are from the Desolation kiosk.

Description: This is a great hike in early fall with the cooler hiking weather. It is definitely a physical challenge, but your rewards are the great views (even better than from Mt. Tallac) and the right to say you did it (I did it!). The peak is 9235', so it will be cool and windy at the top. Pack some extra clothing to accommodate the cooler conditions you can expect at the peak. A trail map is also great to have for identifying the various peaks and lakes you will see. Definitely bring your camera for recording your feat. There will be little water for your dog along this route, so carry plenty for the pooch and yourself.

The first part of the hike is 3.5 miles of challenging ascent, gaining 2280'. Starting from the trailhead, you walk along a shaded dirt path, switch backing your way through a fir and pine forest. After about 20 minutes, you reach a crest and have a great view to the southeast of the barren slopes of Sierra-At-Tahoe Ski Resort.

Continuing your climb, in 30 minutes you reach another crest. You will be able to see Lover's Leap to the southwest and the Carson Range to the south, including on a clear day a look at the Two Sentinels on Thunder Mountain. For a short time, you descend a little toward Tamarack Creek that you will not cross (but a good place to let your dog visit for a drink). Instead, you head north uphill, sometimes over very steep parts, and then enter into Desolation Wilderness.

From the Wilderness Boundary, you continue your climb. There is an overlook area for viewing the distant Crystal Range and Pyramid Peak to the northwest. Your trail flattens temporarily at about 2.4 miles and now you face two trail options. Your first option is to continue straight here on what newer maps prescribe as the correct path. Your other choice is turn right onto an old trail that hikers have resurrected in recent years, making it the more obvious path to choose. Your distance will be about the same.

Option #1 - Continuing Straight:

If you continue straight here, you hike along a side-hill ridge as you skirt through a hillside meadow. You then resume your climb, finally cresting after the end of 3.4 miles. At the summit, look for a pile of rocks and sticks marking the trail to Ralston Peak to the right (east). There are no signs or posts to help you. If you miss this turn, then you will start descending down toward Lake of the Woods. From the turning point, you now have 0.7 miles and a climb of 435' to Ralston Peak. Along the way, there are places to stop for great views to the northwest of Lake Aloha and Lake of the Woods, with peaks of the Crystal Range in the distance. To the north, you can see Lake Tahoe. While making your way toward Ralston Peak on the sometimes-faint trail, you should turn back often to record visual landmarks for your return trip (or place some markers for yourself). It is very easy to get off-trail on the return.

The trail ends at the base of the peak and its rocky foot. You can carefully traverse these rocks (some loose) and gain your way to the top. Directly below the peak, you see the three Ralston Peak basin lakes,

Tamarack, Ralston, and Cagwin. To the east of these, you have a clear view of Upper and Lower Echo Lakes. Directly across the vast canyon, you see Mt. Tallac, taller at 9735', and you can barely see Gilmore Lake just below it. Between you and Mt. Tallac, you can see Grass Lake. Cup Lake is to the southeast. You will see Lake Tahoe and a portion of Fallen Leaf Lake in the distant northeast. To the northeast is Lake Aloha with its dam opened this time of year, making for something of a mud flat for your vista rather than the manmade lake itself.

After your full feast of the views, start carefully back to the main trail. Make sure to find your visual landmarks on the way. There are "ducks" marking a path down toward Lake of the Woods – you do not want to follow these. Your path is mostly without "ducks", so look instead for those visual reminders. Your trail is more directly heading west at this point, always keeping Pyramid Peak directly in front of you. If you sense you are heading down toward Lake of the Woods, then stop and retrace your path uphill to find the correct route. Once you hit the main trail, it will be an easy trip back down to the trailhead. You can figure about 3.0 hours for the climb up and only 2.5 hours for the trip back.

Option #2 – Turning Right

If you turn to the right, you will be on the old trail, now the more heavily used choice by hikers once again. You will climb 600' in the next mile before reaching a junction in the trail. The trail to your left will take you 175' up to Ralston Peak in 0.6 miles. If you continue straight at the junction, you will be on a vague, old trail on route to hidden Cup Lake. If you wish to try a visit to Cup, consider just reaching a vista point to view the small crater-like lake, rather than dropping down the 200' to the lake itself. The climb back up its rocky, sloping banks could be quite treacherous, if not impossible. You may be able to get a view of Cup from the Ralston Peak vantage point and be happy enough with that. Just look to the southeast while at the peak for a glimpse and photo.

Just as with Option #1, be sure to retrace your steps precisely to return to the Ralston Peak Trail and a downhill hike back to your vehicle.

45 – Tallac Historic Site and Taylor Creek Visitor Center Camp Richardson, CA

Difficulty: 1
Distance: 2.5 miles one-way (easier options exist)
Elevation: This is a flat walk with a 15' change in elevation overall

Directions: At the 'Y' in South Lake Tahoe on Highway 50, continue straight on Highway 89 in the direction of Tahoe City. Go 1.4 miles and park on the right shoulder near Marker #46). The bike trail is a little further in from the road on the right. Start on the bike trail going left in the direction of Camp Richardson.

Description: This is an enjoyable walk, at times on a bike trail, and at others on an unpaved walking trail. You visit the Tallac Historic Site with refurbished old estates to tour, gardens to stroll, and weekend festivities to enjoy in summer months. You walk to the Taylor Creek Visitor Center with a 0.5-mile loop Rainbow Trail and an underground stream chamber for viewing underwater wildlife.

Starting on the paved bike trail, after 0.2 mile, you will find a spur trail leading away toward the lake. You can take this to a wildlife sanctuary, a marsh, and a view of Tahoe Keys. At Pope Beach (no dogs allowed at Pope Beach), you need to return to the bike trail to reach Camp Richardson. In town, there are numerous stores and eateries, as well as a trolley car. Continue on the bike trail through the town until you see the sign directing you to the Tallac Historic Site to the right. Take this paved trail to reach the park.

At the Tallac Historic Site, you can stroll past three refurbished estates: Valhalla, Pope, and Baldwin. Also on the grounds are the servants quarters furnished in the style of the early 1900's. You can also look into an old dairy, guest cottages, and a kitchen (unless boarded for the season). Two old boathouses remain (now theatres), along with a barn, and garage. From the boathouses, you can access the beach (dogs allowed). Numerous benches and picnic tables are available on the grounds, as well as an arboretum and pond, and a native plants garden.

Continuing in the same direction, from Tallac, you can pick up the Tallac Historic Site Trail from the Tallac parking area (this is not the same parking area you passed on your way into the park; it is on the opposite side of the park). Walk about 15 minutes away from the lake toward the bike trail to reach the Taylor Creek Visitor Center.

At the Visitor Center, you can purchase books, maps, and postcards. There is a short Smokey's Trail for children to learn about fire safety. Opposite the Visitor Center, you will find the Forest Tree Trail, an interpretive loop identifying trees and wildlife common in the forest. You can also find staff to answer any questions, and perhaps join a naturalist walk. From the Visitor Center, pick up the Rainbow Trail for a self-guided walk on this signed trail. The Rainbow Trail, lined with informational signs explaining the ecosystem, follows along Taylor Creek and leads to an underground stream viewing chamber (no dogs allowed in the chamber). The trail continues from here as a loop, taking you back to the Visitor Center. In October, you can see Kokanee salmon spawning and forest service personnel are available throughout the month to answer any questions.

After touring on the Rainbow Trail, follow the 0.5-mile interpretive Lake of the Sky Trail to dog-friendly Kiva Beach. Here your dog can find plenty of dogs to play with, run on the beach, and jump in the water to retrieve sticks or enjoy a swim. This is a great year round destination for your pooch, especially on hot, summer days. When you are ready to leave, walk past the Visitor Center towards Highway 89 to find the bike trail for your return walk.

Throughout the summer, starting Memorial Day weekend, they offer numerous activities, for both children and adults. In 2016, a sampling of events included a Dixie swing night, the Tahoe Improv Players, "Who's Afraid of Virginia Wolf", artists in residence, and various music events.

You can check www.valhallatahoe.com, or phone (530) 541-4975, to see what the scheduled activities are for the day you plan to visit. At the Baldwin Estate, you can get maps and information and purchase tickets for touring the Pope Estate. In October, the prime activity here is watching the Kokanee spawning as the tours and events have ended for the season. We have fun visiting here throughout the year.

Less Ambitious Option: For those with physical limitations, you can park at both the Tallac Historic Site and the Taylor Creek Visitor Center (Marker #48 on Highway 89) and enjoy touring both. This will eliminate the walk along the bike trail, and most of the mileage.

46 – Mt. Tallac via Floating Island Lake
Camp Richardson, CA

Difficulty: 5
Distance: 1.7 miles to Floating Island Lake
2.5 miles to Cathedral Lake
4.7 miles to Mt. Tallac
Elevation: 3300' elevation gain

Directions: In South Lake Tahoe, at the junction of Highways 50 and 89, continue straight on Highway 89. Continue 3.9 miles and make a left turn in the direction of Mt. Tallac Trailhead (at 3.2 miles you will see the Lake Tahoe Visitor Center on the right where you can pick up a Wilderness Day Permit; however, usually these are also available at the trailhead).

Follow the signs pointing to Mt. Tallac, first a left at 0.4 mile and then a right at a second fork. From here, drive 0.4 mile to the trailhead parking area. This is a popular summer hike and the parking can be full in peak season, but in late October, there should plenty of spaces.

Description: This is an uphill hike with a lot of elevation gain. In addition, the footing is difficult with many loose rocks to ascend. You should plan on more time than normal to make the 4.7 miles to the peak of Mt. Tallac. My normal mountain hiking time is 2.0 miles per hour, but on this hike, on the steeper parts my time was closer to 1.0 mile per hour. Be sure to bring along a good camera and a map of Desolation Wilderness and seriously consider hiking poles for balance.

From the parking area, you will start your ascent with a sweat-breaking 250-foot rocky climb before slightly leveling. After another 100 feet of climbing, you will emerge with a great view of Fallen Leaf Lake and Lake Tahoe. After 0.5 mile, the trail leaves the ridge and you head away from Fallen Leaf Lake and another ridge. Leaving that ridge, the hike is less rocky and you pass a stream. At 1.7 miles, you will reach the Wilderness border and Floating Island Lake just beyond. Occasionally, mats of grass break away from the lake's shore, forming floating island mats, giving the lake its name.

Leaving Floating Island, continue on the trail 0.8 mile to Cathedral Lake. Just before reaching the lake, there will be a post marking a trail down to Fallen Leaf Lake. Continue on to the smaller Cathedral Lake, named appropriately for the cathedral-like rock mass above its western shore, known as Cathedral Peak. Take a nice rest here, because soon you will start the steepest part of the climb. You are now over half way to Mt. Tallac, but have only gained a third of the elevation at this point so the climb ahead will be much steeper.

You leave Cathedral Lake in the direction of Cathedral Peak. Climbing above the lake, you have great views back down to Cathedral and Fallen Leaf Lakes. The climb here is difficult, but it will shortly worsen. Look for rock "ducks" marking the trail, ascending to a point where you can see the path ahead climbing steeply up the rocky face of Mt. Tallac's southeast ridge. This part of the trail is extremely steep, almost vertical at times, and very slippery with small rocks. Take your time making your way up. If your calves start to hurt, then concentrate on planting your foot with the heel rather than the toes. This should help to stretch the calves.

When you finally reach the top of this section, you will hike out a short distance to a trail. You will go right here, but make a note that there is also a trail going to your left. On your return trip, be sure to remember this spot so you do not continue hiking down the slope. You will need to make a left turn on your return to attain the correct trail, so look back now and remember this area and make a mental note of the return route.

You have now completed the steepest portion of the hike, gaining another 1000', but ascents remain, eventually gaining another 1000'. Your reward is the great views to the west of distant peaks of the Crystal Range and lakes lying below them. Toward the end of the climb, you will reach a junction with the trail leading down to Gilmore Lake. Turn right here for the final 0.2 mile and 200' vertical gain to reach the peak of Mt. Tallac.

From this point, the views are great both to the east with Lake Tahoe in site, and to the west down to Gilmore Lake, Susie Lake, and Lake Aloha. Hopefully, you have packed in a good map of Desolation Wilderness to help you to identify the distant peaks, mountain ranges, and lakes. While the trek was strenuous, the rewarding views make it all worthwhile.

Note that you are at 9735' at the peak of Mt. Tallac and the weather can be changeable. You will want warm clothing with you and rain gear. Do not attempt this hike if thunderstorms are in the forecast. It will be very windy at the peak. Also, remember to take time on the hike back down because the steep sections will be extremely slippery. If you start to fall, try to land on your rear to avoid injuring a wrist or a knee. Take all precautions to make this a safe journey.

47 – Lake Margaret
Kirkwood, CA

Difficulty: 2
Distance: 2.5 miles to Lake Margaret
Elevation: 200' gain

Directions: From Highway 50 in Pollock Pines, take Exit 60 for Sly Park Road As you exit the freeway, you will take a right onto Sly Park Road and continue 4.6 miles. Here make a left onto Mormon Emigrant Trail and go about 25 miles to its end at Highway 88. Make a left and head east on 88 to Kirkwood.

Continue past the ski resort on your right and the Kirkwood Cross Country and Snowshoe Center on your left. The next left (0.1 mile from the Cross Country center) is the entrance to the parking area for Lake Margaret. This turn is 11.2 miles from the junction of Mormon Emigrant and Highway 88. Driving west on Highway 88, this entrance is 5.0 miles beyond the Carson Pass Ranger Station. There is ample parking here, but it can get crowded in the afternoons. Overflow parking is available just below the trailhead adjacent to the Cross Country Center chalet. From the overflow, you walk across the small stream and straight up a small hill to join the official trail.

Description: The hike into Lake Margaret is just 2.5 miles, making it one of the easiest hikes to an alpine lake in the Sierra. This is a scenic hike through various habitats, with streams, marshes, aspen groves, and granite rocks. There are log crossings at various points, but if you wear hiking sandals, you can easily wade through the water to avoid the logs. The trail is well marked with signs, blazes on trees (blazes are obvious scars on the tree's trunk due to removal of a strip of the bark, slightly above eye level), and "ducks" marking the way over rocky areas where the trail disappears. There are numerous spur trails to fool you at times, but if you look ahead for the next marker, you can easily stay on the wider main trail.

Starting from the parking area you will see the trailhead sign and start a nice 100'. Quickly the sounds of running water and singing birds replace the noise from the highway. You will reach water quickly and can look over a cliff at a stream below. At 0.5 mile, you will see a spur trail on your left taking you to a peaceful stream and meadow area. The main trail goes to the right here.

At 0.75 mile, the trail borders a large rock wall. The main trail goes to the left here away from the wall. There was a signpost to indicate the trail, but it was broken the last time I visited. Shortly you will come to one of the log crossings with an extremely wide log for your use. From here, the trail starts uphill and then around a large rock formation. The trail goes to the left around the rocky area and arrives at a small pond (may be dry).

Log crossing after an early snowfall

From the pond, the trail goes to the right, keeping the pond on your left. You will find blazes on trees, and "ducks" to mark your way. At 1.5 miles, you will arrive at a larger pond. Continue now across rocks and through a grove of large aspens to the final water crossing. After making the crossing, look for the trail to your right taking you uphill. You have a short ascent over rocks to arrive at the plateau and then an easy walk into the lake. It takes about 1.5 hours to reach the lake. Relax and enjoy the lake before your return trip, remembering you have that 100' ascent at the end back to your car. On your trip out, look for a great view of 10,381' Round Top Peak in the distance.

This is a great hike for your dog, with lots of water and open space to enjoy. Try to start early in the morning to avoid the afternoon crowds. In a year with low rainfall, and no late snow, you can come here in mid-June and enjoy the greenery and fresh wildflowers. In October, you get to enjoy greater solitude and some wonderful fall colors along the streams, in the meadows, and with the groves of aspen.

48 – Round and Bryan Meadows

There are two options for reaching Bryan Meadows, starting from different trailheads.

Sayles Canyon
El Dorado National Forest

Difficulty:	4 (3 if you turn around at Round Meadow)
Distance:	10.6-mile loop
	3.75 miles to Round Meadow
	5.25 miles to the PCT
	6.1 miles to Bryan Meadow
Elevation:	1805' overall gain
	1085' to Round Meadow
	1735' to the PCT

Warning: Bikes are not allowed on the PCT, so you cannot legally do the entire loop on a bike. You can ride to Bryan Meadow and turn around for a challenging mountain-bike outing.

Directions: Head east on Highway 50, going about 45 miles beyond Placerville (3.0 miles beyond Camp Sacramento), and turn right onto Sierra-At-Tahoe Ski Resort Road. Go 1.4 miles on the paved road, and turn right onto a graded dirt/gravel road (unsigned Road 11N09) for another 2.0 miles, ending in a parking circle at the trailhead. Leave the larger horse trailer parking spot for equestrian use.

Description: The Sayles Canyon-Bryan Meadow Trail is lightly used, and yet it is a very rewarding hike with solitude, meadows, views, and a variety of vegetation. For those not wanting to do the long loop, a couple shorter options are available. A good portion of the trail parallels creeks, providing water for your dog; however, the section from Round Meadow to the PCT is dry, so be sure to carry some dedicated water for your pooch.

The trail starts at the sign located at the far end of the parking circle. Shortly, the trail meets Bryan Creek and crosses it several times. In the first 0.7 miles, you steadily gain 375' before a slight rest, followed by another, more gradual, 120' rise in the next 0.4 miles. Here, after 1.1 miles, you come to a trail marker, indicating Round Meadow to the right and Bryan Meadow straight on the main trail. Go right here in the direction of Round Meadow to do the entire loop.

The trail is pleasant now, mostly level, and cooled by the shade of the forest. In 0.3 miles, and a trail of ferns, flowerless columbine and lupine, and a number of diverse plants we were unfamiliar with, you reach one of the Sayles Canyon creeks, with its riparian vegetation, dominated by aspen. This late in the season, the flowers are sparse, but you may still find some purple daisies, thistle, paintbrush, and an occasional lupine with a late-season purple flower. Opposite the creek side of the trail, the canyon floor fills with a sea of white boulders.

Aspen in the fall

The creek is an easy rock-hop this late in the season. Over the next 1.6 miles, you gain another 465' on the rocky trail. At times, the trail can be difficult to read, but the occasional "duck" helps to guide you. Take extra care to look ahead for markers so you do not lose the trail. The trail edges along the Sayles Canyon Creek, and in another 0.75 miles and 125' gain, you will reach Round Meadow.

A tall range (8915' high) of impressive rocks borders the southern section of Round Meadow. This is a pleasant lunch spot, with the meadow now sporting its fall colors. We often make this our turnaround spot. Enjoy a rest here, because once you leave, you will be starting the most strenuous climb of the loop. You gain a difficult 650' over the next 1.5 miles before reaching the intersection with the PCT (hikers doing the Tahoe Rim Trail or the Tahoe-Yosemite Trail also share this portion of the PCT).

Wild Gooseberry on trail to Round Meadow

The PCT is a hiker's super highway, and busy most of the year. At this time of the season, all of the "through" hikers (making the trek from Mexico to Canada) are long gone and into the last leg of the journey in Washington. Nights are cold now for most, but you will have a short break in your solitude nevertheless as you do the next portion of the loop along the PCT with its occasional backpacker. At the intersection, to the right you would go in the direction of Showers Lake. To the left, you go in the direction of Echo Summit, and a continuation of the loop.

Going left on the PCT, you climb just another 70' before reaching the high point of the loop. The remainder of the trail will be mostly downhill. You will be on the PCT for 0.9 miles before reaching the next marker at the eastern edge of Bryan Meadow. At the marker, the main trail goes straight in the direction of Echo Summit. A lesser trail veers slightly to the left in the direction of Highway 50. Take this left trail here and start your walk through the large, colorful, Bryan Meadow.

This portion of the loop takes you along the northern edge of the meadow. Avoid spurs taking you to the center of the meadow. Midway, there is a post identifying the meadow. Stay in the direction of the post and straight along the meadow's edge. The trail is faint in spots, with the spurs seeming to be the main trails, but continue to go along the meadow's perimeter.

After leaving the meadow, the trail starts a serious descent, but the many switchbacks help to minimize the downhill efforts. After dropping 775' in 2.0 miles, you reach a log crossing over Bryan Meadow's creek. The log is split, so there is a slanted section, but not too difficult to accomplish. Continuing on the trail, in another 1.4 miles you return to the original trail split for the two meadows. Now you have just the final 1.1 miles back to the trailhead, with opportunities for great views of the distant Pyramid Peak (9983').

Share with: Bikers (no bikes on any PCT portions) and equestrians.

Bryan Meadow via Echo Summit

Directions: You can also hike to Bryan Meadow by parking nearer to Echo Summit where the PCT emerges before crossing Highway 50 to continue at Echo Lakes. Heading west on Highway 50, turn right into the Adventure Mountain Sno-Park just west of the summit. There is a small, free parking area outside the park (closed for the season).

Description: Head away from the highway to the trail where you will want to head on the arm going to your left (the trail to your right takes you .07 miles west before crossing Highway 50 and continuing another 1.5 miles to Echo Lakes).

The trail heading to your left will take you south and in 1.0 mile and a climb of 133', you will reach Benwood Meadow and travel among large Lodgepole pines. Continuing in this direction another 2.9 miles and a gain of 1000', you reach the junction for Bryan Meadow. With this second trailhead parking possibility, you can plan a hike with cars at either end from Echo Summit down to the parking at Sayles Canyon or from Echo to the Meiss Country parking.

November

This can be the best month to visit mountain trails with the cool weather and diminishing numbers of visitors to the trail. A slight dusting of snow will only enhance the experience. If serious snow threatens, however, consider the lower elevation Codfish Creek Falls trip instead.

View of Fannette Island from Upper Eagle Falls Trail

49 – Codfish Creek Falls Trail
North Fork American River
Weimar, CA

Difficulty: 1
Distance: 1.7 miles to falls
Elevations: Relatively flat trail with 150' elevation gain
Features: 40' waterfall, good family hike

Directions: Take I-80 10 miles east of Auburn, to the second Weimar exit – Weimar Cross Road. Turn right onto Ponderosa Way for 5.7 miles and you will come to the Ponderosa Bridge crossing the North Fork American River. Do not cross this bridge, but turn around and park along the river's side of the road. The trail starts beyond the parking area, going downstream on the north side of the river (again do not cross the bridge to reach the trailhead).

Warnings: *The last 2.4 miles of Ponderosa Way is a graded dirt road descending to the river bottom, and depending on the weather, it can be a rough, slow drive. A 4-wheel drive or high-clearance vehicle is recommended. If there have been recent rains to make the dirt muddy, try this trail later after the road has time to dry.*

Description: Codfish Creek Falls is a trail everyone can easily enjoy, including small children. The only exception would be for someone with balance issues since parts of the trail are narrow and with steep drop-offs. By doing this trail in November, you avoid the poison oak reaching across the narrow sections, but be reminded that even in its dormant stage you can have an allergic reaction if you come in contact.

It is also an interpretive trail with 14 trail markers pointing out native plants, trees, and wildflowers, and spots for possibly seeing or hearing birds along the river. It is best to acquire a brochure to improve your walk (details in the notes below). If you cannot procure a pamphlet, these are the features at the marker posts: 1 – Manzanita; 2 – Canyon

Live Oak; 3 – Dipper possible sighting in the river, or a Merganser, a river duck; 4 – California Bay Laurel and Dutchman's Pipevine; 5 – Buck Brush, Buckeye, and Toyon; 6 – Interior Live Oak and Goldback Fern; 7 – Redbud, 8 – Black Oak; 9 – Ponderosa Pine; 10 – Grey Pine; 11 – Various wildflowers (spring only) such as Lupine, Popcorn Plant, California Poppy, Fiddleneck, Brodiaea, Shooting Star, Larkspur, and Lace Pod; 12 – Douglas Fir and Pacific Madrone; 13 – Birds such as the elusive but vocal Hutton's Vireo; 14 – White Alder.

The first mile follows along the river before bending away to the right to reach Codfish Creek in another 0.7 mile. At the creek, you will find the falls, wonderful rocks and pools of water, and Marker #14. This is a great picnic and photography spot. There is also a spur trail available to take you to the top of the falls (worth the effort). You will find this spur a short distance back on the main trail as it takes off up the hill.

On your return hike, take time to follow one of the side trails down to the river to enjoy the scenery. Across the river, you can see remnants from the dredge mining of long ago. In November, the serenity of fall replaces the busy springtime here at the falls. You sacrifice seeing the falls at their fullest in November, and you miss the wildflower display, but you avoid the poison oak and the many fellow hikers – so many that it a leashed experience for your dog in the busy months. We have visited here in both the spring and the fall, and definitely enjoy the fall the best for a relaxing day at the river.

Notes: A brochure detailing what you can see at each of the trail markers is not always available at the trailhead. You may want to stop first in Auburn (501 El Dorado St.) to pick one up (or call at 530-885-4527). If their office is closed, you may find a brochure at the California Welcome Center 13411 Lincoln Way (also in Auburn 530-887-2111).

50 – Grouse, Hemlock, and Smith Lakes
Wrights Lake Recreation Area

Difficulty: 4

Distance: 2.1 miles to Grouse

                   2.6 miles to Hemlock

                   3.1 miles to Smith

Elevation: 1740' gain from trailhead to Smith Lake

Directions: On Highway 50 in Fresh Pond, make the left turn to Mill Run Ranger Station to pick of a day use permit for Desolation Wilderness (they will not be available at the trailhead in November). Back on Highway 50, heading east, you will continue to Kyburz and then 4.8 miles beyond to the left turn onto Wrights Road.

Go 8.1 miles on Wrights Road into the Wrights Lake Recreation Area. Turn right at the Stop sign and go 1.0 mile down the narrow road to the Twin Lakes Trailhead Parking Area. This is the off-season, so there will be plenty of parking.

Description: I like doing this more difficult hike in November, with the cooler weather making it more pleasurable. If snow threatens, then postpone doing this trip.

Starting from the parking area, walk down the road and past the service gate to find the Loop Trail starting on your right and the Twin Lakes information board. Follow the Loop Trail 0.4 mile to the signed trail for Twin, Grouse, Island, and Hemlock Lakes going to the right.

From here, you start a 140' ascent before reaching a saddle. Then you ascend another 150' to emerge at a trail of rock slabs, often difficult to follow. Keep the Grouse Lake's outlet creek on your left, climbing another 170'. Within 1.0 mile and another 100', you will reach the wilderness boundary. Shortly thereafter, you come to a trail post indicating Grouse Lake to the right and Twin Lake to the left. Follow in the direction of Grouse Lake.

The trail starts over rock slabs, forcing you to look ahead for rock "ducks" marking your path. The trail then veers right as you ascend a gully. The trail flattens for a while, then climbs steeply, ending at the Grouse Lake outlet creek. You need to cross the creek to find the trail on the other side and then continue your climb. You will have gained another 630' to reach Grouse Lake. Grouse is a pretty lake, good for swimming in August and fishing in November.

Grouse Lake with a dusting of snow

If bad weather threatens, then you can make Grouse your turnaround. Of the three lakes, Grouse is the most picturesque and has the best shoreline for picnicking. If you choose to continue forward to the other two lakes, be reassured that the most difficult parts of the hike are behind you.

The trail continues along Grouse's northern shore, and then shortly past the lake, it veers left, uphill another 240', in a northeast direction reaching smaller Hemlock Lake in 0.5 mile. From Hemlock, the trail follows its western shore in a southeastern direction another 0.5 mile and another 310' to Smith Lake. The trail in to Smith Lake is difficult to follow in sections so you must choose your trail carefully. If enough snow has already fallen this season, you will not be able to make your way to Smith Lake safely.

If you can reach Smith Lake, you will be rewarded with its clear water, good fishing including golden trout, and great views down to Wrights Lake, and even to Union Valley Reservoir in the distant Crystal Basin Recreation Area. Enjoy the journey downhill on your return.

Smith Lake

51 – Thunder Mountain
Amador Ranger District
El Dorado National Forest

Difficulty: 4
Distance: 1.5 miles to Two Sentinels
          3.6 miles to Thunder Mountain
Elevation: 750' gain to Two Sentinels
          1570' gain to Thunder Mountain at 9408'

Directions: On Highway 88, continue east 10 miles beyond the junction with Mormon Emigrant Trail (you can also take Mormon Emigrant Trail from Highway 50 to Highway 88) to the ample parking area for Thunder Mountain on the south side of the highway. Coming from the westward direction, this trailhead is just past the Carson Spur and 7.3 miles beyond the Carson Pass Ranger Station.

Description: This is a hike featuring a 360-degree view from the top of Thunder Mountain, but the journey getting there is even more amazing. If you have been afraid of getting lost on wilderness trails, then this is the perfect hike for you along a very clear, dirt footpath. Remember to bring water for your dog, since there will be no water source along the trail.

Starting from the parking area, head out on the dirt trail through a pleasant pine forest. You climb 325', at first gradually, then steeply up a hillside of mule ears, lupine, scarlet gilia, and assorted stonecrop to peak at a site populated with solar panels and snow breaks. You immediately start another climb of 425' up to the impressive rock formations called Two Sentinels.

At the second of these two rocks, you can see karabiners left from rock climbers. You also have great views down to Caples Lake in the distance, Kirkwood Meadows, and Kirkwood Lake immediately below. From here, you climb another 100' to Martin Point. You will see signage for a new trail connecting Kirkwood Meadows Ski Resort with the Thunder Mountain Trail.

Continuing straight, now the climbing is more gradual for the next two miles, and where steep you will have switchbacks to make it easier to gain the next 800'. As you approach your destination, you drop 100', and then regain them again.

To reach Thunder Mountain's peak, you need to leave the main trail and take a spur trail to its top. To find this spur trail, continue a short distance down from the trail's crest point, around two curves to a definite drop down point in the trail. Here you should see "ducks" marking the spur trail to the right. Do not continue down the trail here unless you want to join up with the Horse Canyon Trail (taking you to another parking area).

Make your way carefully up the spur trail to the peak to enjoy the 360-degree panorama. Round Top, at 10381', is the tallest point to the east. Expect it to be cool at your 9408' vantage point, and be prepared for changeable weather. On a 100-degree day in Sacramento Valley in August, we experienced a 60-degree day here, with sprinkles and hail at the peak.

On your return trip, be sure to take the same spur trail back to the main trail. If you attempt a shortcut, you will find yourself on loose rocks and steep, dangerous terrain. Enjoy the mostly downhill hike back to the parking area, and the impressive view of the Two Sentinels, seemingly guarding the hill and the other volcanic rocks between them.

Share with: Bikers (bikes allowed but not recommended) and equestrians.

52 – Eagle Falls Trails
Emerald Bay, Lake Tahoe

You can enjoy two hikes at the Eagle Falls area, one on each side of Highway 89.

Directions: From the "Y" in South Lake Tahoe where Highway 50 veers to the right, continue straight on Highway 89 for 8.8 miles (past Camp Richardson) to the Eagle Falls parking area on the left of the highway. At this time of the year, the normal fees are suspended. If you visit earlier in the season, you can still park free alongside the highway rather than driving down into the official fee parking area. I suggest parking along the highway regardless of the fees for an easy cross over the highway later for a view of Lower Eagle Falls.

From Tahoe City, you travel south on Highway 89 about 19.0 miles to the Eagle Falls parking area on your right.

After the hike: If you did not pack a lunch to enjoy at the lake, then visit dog-friendly Burger Lounge just south on Highway 89 past Camp Richardson. They allow dogs in their patio dining area and have a picnic area behind the restaurant as well. In November, they have limited days of operation.

Eagle Lake via Upper Eagle Falls

Difficulty: 2
Distance: 1.3 direct to Eagle Lake, another 0.5 miles to take the loop to Vista Point
Elevation: 435' climb to lake

Description: This is an extremely popular trail in the summer months, with parking difficult to come by, but in November, you should have no problems. If you will be hiking into Eagle Lake, then fill out the Desolation Wilderness Day Pass available at the trailhead.

Eagle Lake

There is a loop trail for a journey to a vista point, and then to a bridge crossing Upper Eagle Falls. Start the loop by staying to the right and climb up to the Vista Point. From here, you can look out to Emerald Bay, Fannette Island, and Lake Tahoe. Behind you is a rock face popular for beginner rock climbers. Continuing the loop, you drop down to the bridge crossing Upper Eagle Falls.

Cross the bridge to pick up the trail to Eagle Lake. You make a steady climb up to the lake on an easy to follow trail. You hear the water from Eagle Creek below you as you make the climb. When you reach a post indicating the trail to Velma Lakes to the left, turn right on the spur trail to reach picturesque Eagle Lake.

On your return trip, after crossing the bridge finish your original loop trail by staying to the right, following alongside the creek. At first, you have rock steps to descend carefully. You then reach a viewing area with benches to look back up toward the falls. This is the best view you will have of Upper Eagle Falls. From here, it is an easy walk back to the parking area.

More Ambitious: From the main trail to Eagle Lake, you could continue on to Middle and Upper Velma Lakes, as well as make a loop to include Fontanillis and Dicks Lake. Bring along a good map of Desolation Wilderness before attempting this approximately 13-mile journey.

Less Ambitious: If you have physical limitations, you can still enjoy a visit to Upper Eagle Falls. Starting from the trailhead, take the left portion of the loop trail. If you can make it up two flights of steep stairs, you will be able to make it to the viewing area for the upper falls. This is the best viewing spot and is well worth your efforts.

Vikingsholm and Lower Eagle Falls

Difficulty: 2

Distance: 0.9 miles to Vikingsholm

1.2 miles to Lower Eagle Falls

Elevation: 400' drop to beach from parking area

Warning: Do not be tempted to carve your initials into the soft bark of the aspens along the trail. Not only is this vandalism, but it harms the trees and ruins the beauty of nature for fellow hikers.

Directions: From the Eagle Falls parking area described above, travel just 0.2 miles north on Highway 89 to the Vikingsholm parking area on the right.

Description: This is a busy tourist site throughout the summer, with tours of the Scandinavian-styled mini-castle called Vikingsholm available throughout the season. The site officially closes after September 30 and you will find the lower windows and doors boarded up, but you can visit the park year-round. By mid-November, you can enjoy a trip here without many other visitors, and the parking is free. If you want a tour, you will need to return in the busy summer months (no dogs allowed in the summer season), and pay for parking and the inside tour (separate fees).

From the parking area, you can read about the history of Vikingsholm on some informational kiosks. Built in 1929 as a summer retreat for a wealthy Chicagoan, great care was taken to preserve the natural surroundings. From the kiosks, you start on the closed road down to the beach and the buildings.

There is one large switchback to break up the descent. Toward the bottom, a paved road heads to the left in the direction of D.L. Bliss State Park. You continue straight here. At the end of your descent, you come first to the old gardener's cottage on your left, and the main house and Visitor's Center ahead of you. The nicely groomed beach area is dotted with picnic tables, and you can walk out onto a pier. In mid-November, you may be treated to a dusting of snow decorating the scene. Your view out to Emerald Bay includes a close-up of Lake Tahoe's only island, Fannette Island, used for tea parties by the summer visitors to Vikingsholm in its early days.

Vikingsholm itself sports some beautiful woodwork, with large pillars with decorative carvings, a wood-framed dormer window with stained glass, and unique wooden downspouts. Parts of the roof contain a sprinkler system for plantings. Multiple chimneys and castle-like turrets dominate. Be sure to walk around the entire structure and take pictures from the different angles.

From the Visitor's Center (closed for the season), locate the start of the Eagle Falls Trail taking you to lower Eagle Falls. The falls are at their fullest in June and early July, but still worth seeing later in the year. If you want to return earlier in the busy tourist season, remember that you will pay to park and the Forest Service does not allow dogs (you also pay for a tour inside of Vikingsholm). If you take your dog in mid-November, be sure to keep it leashed and have a bag to pick up any poop – you could still get a warning from a ranger, but if you leave poop on the beach, you can expect a ticket. Scoop it or ticket! If you come later in the winter, you may need to bring along some snowshoes.

Lower Eagle Falls in the spring

More Ambitious: If you stand on the pier facing Vikingsholm, look to your right for a sign for the Rubicon Trail. You can walk along the shore here, making your way to Emerald Point (1.5 miles) at the start of the bay, or further on to D. L. Bliss State Park, ending at Rubicon Point (additional 3.5 miles).

53 – Caples Lake Trails
Carson Pass Management Area
Mokelumne Wilderness

You have two trail options at Caples Lake to do on two separate occasions, or after familiarizing yourself with both trails, you can accomplish both in a single loop if you start early enough now that days are shorter.

Warning: *Dogs need to remain leashed in Mokelumne Wilderness*

Directions: Parking for the Emigrant Lake trailhead is at the spillway area of Caples Lake. Heading east on Highway 88, the parking area is on the right side of the highway, just past the Kirkwood Cross Country Ski Center and the Lake Margaret Trail on the left. This is about 12.4 miles beyond the junction with Mormon Emigrant Trail. Heading west from the junction of Highway 89 with Highway 88, you travel past the Carson Pass Ranger Station about 5.0 miles to the parking area for Caples Lake Dam on the left. Both trails described start from this parking area.

Emigrant Lake

Difficulty: 3
Distance: 4.4 miles to Emigrant Lake
Elevation: 900' gain

Description: This hike starts quite leisurely for the first two miles as you follow along Caples Lake's southwestern shoreline, gaining a mere 100'. The majority of your elevation gain is all on the second leg of the journey. This first part is shaded and cool in November, so wear an extra layer of clothing for the trip. As you go along the shoreline, minor trails take you down to the lake. Always keep to the upper trail at these splits to remain on the main Emigrant Lake Trail. After 1.3 miles, you reach a junction signed to the right for Historic Emigrant Trail and Emigrant Lake straight. Stay straight here in the direction of Emigrant Lake. Ahead of you, beyond Caples Lake, you have a great view of Round Top (10,381') in the distance, and of the closer Black Butte. If the season has early snowfall, then Round Top will be spectacular.

In another mile, you leave Caples Lake and start a more serious climb. The trail follows along the outlet stream for Emigrant Lake, and makes several crossings. In November, these crossings may be dry (unless there is early season rainfall) until you get much closer to the lake. At the 2.5-mile mark, you enter a pleasant meadow, with a flat path before continuing your rocky climb. In another 0.5 miles, you find another directional post indicating Kirkwood Meadow to the right. Again, stay straight in the direction of Emigrant Lake. At this point, you have gained 375' of the total 900' elevation gain.

The trail is extremely easy to follow, with a clear footpath and wherever there could be any confusion, you will find ample signage to direct you. The higher that you climb, you may start to get a couple of pools of water in the stream to cool your pooch. At 3.7 miles, you arrive at another stream crossing, easy in November, but probably still with some water.

The final, more serious climb, gains 525' before you arrive at the stream coming from Emigrant Lake. From here, you enjoy a beautiful entrance to the lake along the stream, with your path decorated with fall foliage. Soon, you get a peek at your destination lake, with tall granite borders at the southern end of its sparkling waters, and Covered Wagon Peak to the west.

For the best picnic spot, cross on the spur trail to the right as soon as the lake is in sight. This takes you to the lake's northwestern end, with a flat, rocky area large enough to spread out your picnic. We saw no fish at the lake, but we did see some small brook trout in the stream below the lake.

Share with: Equestrians (no bikes allowed in the wilderness area).

Less Ambitious: just do the first 2.3 miles along Caples Lake and stop at one of the many small beaches

Old Emigrant Road

Difficulty: 3
Distance: 3.3 miles to Kirkwood Meadows
Elevation: 700' gain

Description: Start along the Emigrant Lake Trail described above and hike the 1.3 miles to the intersection with the trail for Historic Emigrant Trail to the right. As you face the sign for this trail, look slightly to your left for the first trail marker at eye level on a tree. You need to find this first marker to get started on the right path.

The next 1.5 miles are amply marked with these "California Trail" signs in the trees. Older markers for Emigrant Road (also marked as the Carson Emigrant Trail) still exist in some trees as well. This is a lightly traveled, pine covered trail, but in surprisingly good condition and easy enough to follow. You start with a tough climb, warming you enough to remove a clothing layer. After some serious climbing, you can relax as you travel next along a flatter path. You have some great views of Round Top throughout this leg.

At the end of this 1.5-mile stretch, you exit Mokelumne Wilderness and come to a dirt service road. Look across the road to find another "California Trail" marker. This next 0.5-mile portion of the old trail has fewer markers, but you should be able to follow the correct path, first up hill, and then gently down to the old Emigrant Valley now occupied by Kirkwood Meadows Ski Resort. As an alternative, you could turn left onto the service road and end up in the valley that way.

Walk down to the dirt service road and look for the Sunrise Ski Lift to your left and the Outback Grill (closed until winter) immediately ahead of you. The Grill has a wood deck and chairs you could use for a lunch break, but we could not get Toots to climb up the metal, grated stairs. There are also picnic tables in the area, but since these were shaded, we opted for a sunny flat rock for our lunch.

You should be able to spot another "California Trail" marker up the road. From there, look far up the gully to see the next marker across the meadow. We stopped here and did not continue along the trail portion called Carson River Route, but according to the map, it would take you up the gully and around Covered Wagon Peak, eventually joining Horse Canyon Trail. The old road originally took you all the way to Placerville. With the shorter November days, it is best to turn around here at Kirkwood. If you want to try the longer journey, return here in September, and be sure to have a good Mokelumne Wilderness map with you.

For the trip back, we found it difficult to find the markers, so we dropped down to the dirt service road and hiked it back to the spot where the trail had crossed the road. It was easy then to follow the markers on the remainder of the journey.

You could make a loop trail, first by doing the trail to Emigrant Lake, and then on the return, take the cutoff trail heading to Kirkwood. This would bring you out to the area you stopped at on the Old Emigrant Road Trail. You could then return on that trail. The cutoff takes less than 10 minutes and then you arrive at Kirkwood. It is best to do both legs individually at first to learn the nuances of the trails, and then do the loop in the future.

Historical Interest: Historical Marker #661 beyond Caples Lake Resort details the history of the Emigrant Trail. In 1848, the trail went down through the meadow that Caples Lake now covers. The trail climbed over the mountains and then descended into Placerville. In 1863, the trail was abandoned and a new, simpler route was created over the Carson Spur.

DECEMBER

With snow looming in the mountains, it is time to return to the foothills and explore some great trails in the cooler weather. Poison oak is dormant (still potentially an allergen), rattlesnakes are resting, and the crowds have vanished. With the hectic holiday season fully upon us, relaxing walks along the river can be soothing.

South Fork American River on Magnolia Ranch Trail

54 – Confluence Trails
Auburn State Recreation Area

Difficulty: 3
Distance: 5.0-mile loop
Elevation: 520' gain, with one 0.5-mile section gaining 350'

Directions: Coming from Auburn on Interstate 80 (I-80), take Highway 49 South and travel 3.3 miles to the bottom of the canyon. Turn right there and cross the Highway 49 Bridge (continuing straight, you would be on Old Foresthill Road). Immediately, find parking off Highway 49 near Gate 150 on the right side of the road.

Coming from Cool and heading North on Highway 49, the roadside parking area will be on your left, just before you would cross the Highway 49 Bridge. This parking area is at the bottom of the river canyon, and known popularly as the "No Hands Bridge" parking (currently free).

Description: This walk takes you along the river, to views of the confluence of the Middle and North Forks of the American River, and sites of bridges – old, new, and in ruins. This is both an historical journey as well as one rich in nature's beauty. You will definitely want to have the Auburn State Recreation Area (ASRA) map (available at local REI stores and the ASRA Park Headquarters) before doing this hike.

Starting from the parking area, walk behind Gate 150 onto the dirt road paralleling the river to the Mountain Quarries Railroad Bridge, also known as No Hands Bridge (from equestrians bravely riding with reins dropped prior to the installation of guardrails on the bridge). Walk across the 170' bridge to find an informational sign telling about the bridge's history. Completed in 1912, Mountain Quarries Company used the bridge, making four 7-mile runs daily to haul limestone to Auburn for thirty years before dismantling its tracks for scrap metal for World War II. The arched construction of this reinforced concrete bridge (the world's largest of its kind when completed) has proven sturdy enough to survive severe flooding throughout the years.

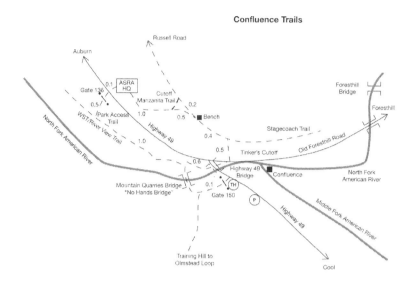

Confluence Trails

From the bridge, locate an uphill spur trail that takes you up toward Highway 49. Follow this trail up 50' to where it begins to parallel the road, taking you back toward and then under the Highway 49 Bridge. Along this stretch of trail, if you look down into the water, you can see the concrete remains of the old Highway 49 Bridge originally constructed in 1948 (remaining until the flood of 1964). Many bridges have spanned the river here over the years (see the notes below for learning more about the history of the bridges).

After walking under the existing Highway 49 Bridge, walk up to the road (Old Foresthill Road), and carefully cross over to the other side. Slightly to your left, just behind the road sign, you can see the continuation of the spur trail, known as Tinker's Cutoff Trail. This trail climbs steeply 360' over the next 0.5 miles, but switchbacks, cool streams, and waterfalls make it bearable.

Tinker's Cutoff Trail ends at the wider Stagecoach Trail – a biker's super highway. Turn left onto historic Stagecoach Trail, established in 1850 and at one time actually used by stagecoaches to transport people between mining towns near what is now Foresthill and Auburn. There were a couple of robberies of stagecoaches on this trail. In about 0.3 miles, you reach a lookout point with a bench. From this point, you can see both No Hands Bridge and the Foresthill Bridge, and below you is a great view down to the river (a better photo shot of the actual confluence is about 200' before reaching this bench). According to the ASRA, had the government completed the Auburn Dam Project then the high water mark of the resulting lake would have been at this bench, and it would have reached the cement piers of Foresthill Bridge as well.

In about 100' from the bench, the Manzanita Trail veers off to the left. You want to take this trail all of the way to the Park Headquarters. If you miss this trail junction, in another 0.2 miles there is a cutoff trail to your left that also takes you down to the Manzanita Trail. If you miss this cutoff trail, and remain on Stagecoach Trail, you will start to see homes in the distant Auburn Hills, ending at the Russell Road trailhead. Turn around and find the cutoff down to the Manzanita Trail. You are on the Manzanita Trail with its numerous seasonal stream crossings about 1.5 miles before reaching the Park Headquarters.

From the park's main entrance road, you can look across the highway to see Gate 136. Carefully cross the road and descend on the Park Access Trail beyond this gate. You drop about 360' in the next 0.5 miles, where the trail ends at the River View Trail (signed Western States Trail or WST). Heading left here, this last mile takes you along the river and back to the Mountain Quarries Railroad Bridge. There are access spots down to the river along this stretch. Also on this portion of the trail, you cross a small stream with a nice waterfall this time of the year, and see numerous concrete remains of railroad footings. Cross back over the bridge to return to your car, completing this enjoyable, historical 5-mile loop.

Share with: Bikers on the Stagecoach and Manzanita Trail portions only (bikes not allowed on Tinker's Cutoff or the Park Access Trail), equestrians on some portions, but no available trailer parking at the described trailhead.

Less Ambitious Option: Park instead at the Russell Road trailhead and enjoy a leisurely walk along the Stagecoach Trail. You will still enjoy all of the views of the bridges and the river in the canyon below without hiking the canyon itself.

55 – Olmstead Loop Trails
Auburn State Recreation Area
Cool, CA

A number of choices emanate from the Olmstead Loop Trailhead, all great options in December. You will not get to enjoy the wildflowers of springtime, but you also avoid the ticks and poison oak this time of the year.

Directions: On Highway 49 in Cool turn on Saint Florian Court at the fire station and find the parking area just behind it. The first level of parking is for cars, and the upper level is for horse trailers. If you are coming from Auburn, it is a right turn on St. Florian Court just before the fire station and the Stop sign. Coming from Coloma, make a left turn just after the Stop sign in Cool and the fire station.

If you do not have an annual State Parks Pass and do not wish to pay the $10.00 parking fee, another option is to park just off Aaron Cool road in a large dirt area. From here, you carefully cross Highway 49 and walk through a break in the fence line to start on the loop trail. Aaron Cool is the first road north of the fire station and the parking is just across the highway from the trail. The following three hiking suggestions all start here.

Olmstead Loop
Knickerbocker Trail

Difficulty: 2
Distance: 7.9-mile loop
Elevation: Rolling trail with two steep ascents of 130' and 270'

Warnings: *Share the trail with mountain bikers and equestrians – always yield to equestrians. If you do this hike in the spring, be sure to check your pooch for ticks.*

Description: This is a fun hike with lots of wildlife to see, along with vernal pools and a couple of creek crossings. Additionally, great views across the American River Canyon and the foothills will award you.

You are going to do this loop in reverse of the marked order (so you will start at the 9.0-mile marker instead of in the 0.0 direction). You will be going in a counter-clockwise direction. Going in the prescribed clockwise direction, I always get lost due to the pond covering the trail in the first mile. Starting in the reverse direction, if parked at the fire station you cross Saint Florian Court and pick up the trail on the other side of the road. If you park at Aaron Cool, then cross the highway and start the trail in a counterclockwise direction.

At first, you will parallel Highway 49, but in 0.25 mile (less from Aaron Cool), you will turn away from its traffic and start to enjoy the rolling hills with 50' "ups and downs", passing the marker for Quarry Trail to the right. In less than 0.5 mile, the Olmstead Loop veers to the right (you will see the trail marker on its path). You will stay straight here, making a little shortcut. For the next 0.5 mile, continue along this shortcut, taking in the tree-lined trail of oaks, passing an old shack and a pond, and then rejoining the loop. Turn left here to continue the loop.

Now you will pass by some rock outcroppings on your left and then come to the 6.5-mile marker for the trail. Soon the trail curves to your right and starts descending to Salt Creek (avoid the narrow spur trails, staying on the wider actual trail). Along the way down, you will come to a nice water spot for your dog. If you look to the left, you will see a pond also. The pond can be a little murky, but my dog likes running in it nevertheless. Continuing on, you reach Salt Creek (not impressive). From the creek crossing, it is a 270-foot ascent, passing by a trail on the right signed Salt Creek Loop (this option is described later).

As you continue along the loop, you will see remnants of ranches that existed before the government took the land for public use for the Auburn Dam Project. The U.S. Bureau of Reclamation now owns the land and the California Park System administers it. The trail was formerly called the Knickerbocker Trail before Dan Olmstead organized bikers to establish a trail to be enjoyed by hikers, bikers, and equestrians together.

Enjoy the rolling hills and the views across the canyon. You will descend once more, down to Knickerbocker Creek. This is a good resting spot, with a loud flow of water, and pools to splash in. After your rest, there is a 130' ascent through a pine forest. You will find mile markers at every 0.5 mile and the trail is easy to follow (avoid spurs and stay on the dirt road) until the last mile when the trail marker leads you left into a marsh. You need to stay straight instead to go around the water. You will find a bridge to your left to help you cross over the water. Looking ahead, you will again see the trail and be able to follow it back to the parking area.

Now that you know the trail's nuances, the next time you visit here you can do the hike in the prescribed clockwise direction, starting at mile 0.0. You should be able to bypass the path into the pond successfully, and make your way around the loop following the trail markers. Look for the marker for the short cut, or else you will add another mile to the loop.

Going in this direction, the ascents from the Knickerbocker and Salt Creek are much easier. If you return in the spring, be sure to bring a camera, because you will see a variety of wildflowers on this hike. Look for the illusive Red Maid that only opens on a sunny day. Bring your wildflower book to help with identifying the various species here.

Less Ambitious Option: Try the trail in its clockwise direction and get lost just as I do after a mile when you reach the marsh. You will see a trail along the right of the marsh that will meander a bit and take you back to the parking area. You will still be able to enjoy the scenery doing this shorter hike.

Share with: Bikers and horses

Pointed Rocks Trail to No Hands Bridge Olmstead Loop

Difficulty: 3
Distance: 6.5-mile loop
Elevation: 1000'elevation change, but generally a rolling hike except for steep 800' descent and then the return ascent

Warning: 0.9- mile steep descent

Description: I believe this is the most scenic route via "No Hands Bridge." If you were to do this hike in the reverse direction, it would rate a '5' in difficulty. You will be treated with some great vistas and perfect trail conditions in December.

Start the loop in reverse direction, so cross the street by the fire station (if parked in the trailhead parking) to enter the trail at its actual end (the 9.0-mile mark), or cross Highway 49 to reach the trail (if parked at Aaron Cool). Follow the trail beside Highway 49 for a short while before it heads west away from the road and into the rolling foothills. You will pass four trail junctions on your way to Pointed Rocks. Follow the green State Park post marker at each junction to stay on the Olmstead Loop Trail.

After 1.3 miles, you will see a field of boulders known as Pointed Rocks. Here you can rest and enjoy the Sierra views and the colorful lichen covering on the rocks. As you continue beyond here, the distant views are even more photogenic. Then in a short while, you will come to the junction with Training Hill Trail.

You will leave Olmstead Loop here and take this trail to the right. You will reach a sign warning of a 0.9-mile steep downhill. On the way down, enjoy the coolness of pine cover and great views of Foresthill Bridge, the distant mountains, and the hillside homes in Auburn. Take the descent slowly and enjoy.

At trail's end, you will come to "No Hands Bridge" (local name for Mountain Quarries Railroad Bridge credited to equestrians crossing it with hands off the reins) crossing the North Fork American River and a pleasant resting spot. Just before the bridge, there is a steep spur trail down to the river and a very nice beach for a picnic and a rest. After your lunch, take time to walk across the bridge. There is a marker at the far end giving you historical information about the bridge.

When ready for the return trip, start on the same route from "No Hands Bridge" back up the hill. In a short distance, you will come to a junction. The sign shows Training Hill Trail straight and the Western States Trail (WST) left, with Cool 3.3 miles away. Take the left turn here and continue following signs in the direction toward Cool. The WST trail joins the Wendell T. Robie Trail. Stay on this trail and in the direction of Cool (pass by the junction for Short Cut Trail). For a while, the trail follows the canyon side bordering the highway, and it is noisy and very cool. Then it turns away, and you will reach a more open terrain dotted by deciduous oaks with their leaves turning colors.

At the 7.5-mile state marker, veer left along an old fence line and follow this trail for a short while until you emerge back onto Olmstead Loop. Go left here and retrace your route back to the parking area.

Less Ambitious Option: Just hike to Pointed Rocks and then turn around there. Do not attempt the Training Hill Descent unless you are sure of your balance. Once you return to your car, drive along Highway 49 toward Auburn to the parking area for "No Hands Bridge". This area is opposite the river's side of Highway 49, just before crossing over the river. Walk in to the bridge from here.

More Ambitious: Once your reach "No Hands Bridge", start the route for the Confluence Trail and add 5 miles to your day.

Share with: Horses

Salt Creek Loop Trail
(Formerly Coffer Dam)

Difficulty: 3

Distance: 4.4 miles one-way

Elevation: Easy down to the river and then a strenuous 1000' return climb, broken into one 700' ascent over 1.8 miles, a 100' rise over 0.5 miles, and then 200' over the last 2.1 miles

Description: Skip the Stairmaster and opt instead to break a sweat on the Salt Creek Loop Trail off the Olmstead Loop Trail. This trail is going to take you to the site of the now-abandoned diversion tunnel needed originally for the Auburn Dam Project.

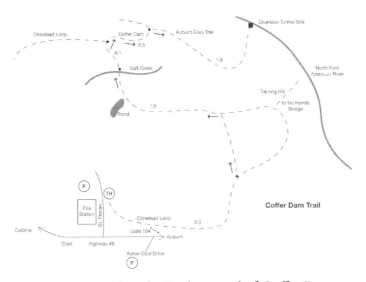

Signage now reads Salt Creek instead of Coffer Dam

Start on the Olmstead Loop, walking in a counterclockwise direction, with your first mile marker at the 8.5 point on the trail. In 0.5 miles, the marked trail veers to the right. There is a shortcut trail here straight ahead that you should take. When you reach the end of the shortcut, continue in the counterclockwise direction on the Olmstead Loop main trail (remember this intersection). The next mile-marker you pick up is the one for 6.5 miles.

Shortly, you will pass by a pond on your left, with levels fluctuating throughout the year depending on the season's rainfall. From the pond, you descend to the crossing at Salt Creek at the 2.0-mile mark of your hike. Salt Creek's crossing will vary in difficulty depending on the seasonal water flows, but most likely just a trickle at this time of the year.

From Salt Creek, it is a short 0.1-mile ascent of 60' to the intersection with the Salt Creek Loop Trail to the right. Take this trail to the right here, leaving the Olmstead Loop. The trail meanders nicely for 0.5 miles before intersecting with the Auburn-Cool Trail. Take this trail to the right and enjoy the next 1.8 miles downhill to the river. Along the way, you pass near a cemented waterway off to your right (you need to leave the trail to see it).

As you approach the river, you see the remaining building and gates of the diversion tunnel system originally built to divert the river water underground at the point of the proposed dam. The federal government abandoned the project for the dam in 1976, and then restoration for the river started in 2003. With the original plan, you could cross the river here and continue to the other side and to Auburn (crossing still shown on maps). Now the only crossing available is at No Hands Bridge, so from here you have to head back on a strenuous uphill climb. Remember to look for your shortcut on the loop after about 3.4 miles on your return trip.

Share with: Bikers and equestrians.

56 – American Canyon Trail
Third Gate
Auburn Lake Trails

Difficulty: 3
Distance: 7-mile loop plus spur side trips
Elevation: 975' climb from river (broken into 200', 345' and 430' sections)

Warning: *Poison oak lines this trail, but at this time of the year, it has no leaves and is less of a problem. However, you can still get an allergic reaction from just the sticks. Stay on the trail, wear long pants and long sleeves, and if you are highly susceptible, do not do the spur trails.*

Directions: From Highway 49 in Cool (8 miles from Auburn and 11 miles from Coloma), turn onto Highway 193 toward Greenwood and Georgetown. Travel 6.1 miles on Highway 193 and turn left onto unsigned Pilgrim Way (this is across the road from the signed Pilgrim Court). Go just 0.2 miles (just short of the gated entrance to Auburn Lake Trails) to find the trailhead on the right. Coming from Georgetown, take Highway 193 in the direction of Greenwood and Cool and travel 6.2 miles to the unsigned Pilgrim Way on the right.

There is limited parking here (about four cars) and room for just a couple cars across the street. Half way between the trailhead and Highway 193, there is room for about another five cars along the roadside. In busy spring and summer, a private property owner .opens up a parking area and charges $8.00, but in the winter, it should be unpopular enough for you to find an available parking space. Although this is a multi-use trail for horses and hikers, there is little room to park a horse trailer here.

Description: This is a nice, scenic loop, with many changes in terrain and features throughout. Starting from the parking area, you start downhill, dropping 430' in the first 0.8 miles. At the bottom of the hill, there is an intersection. Stay straight here (you will be returning on the trail to the right). Reading the trail signs, you learn that there are miles of trails available to you from just this one trailhead.

The next section climbs a little before flattening over the next 2.0 miles. The main trail is well marked, deterring you from any spur trails. Soon, you pick up mile markers every 0.5 miles, starting with the 17.5-mile mark. After a mile on this section, you pick up your first glimpse of the river far below. At about 2.5 miles, you can see a rock shrine erected for Barbara Schoener, a runner killed by a mountain lion in 1994. There is a bench for reflecting across the canyon on the shock of the incident. It is a reminder to us all to practice safety when sharing territory with other animals. Respect their hunting time at dawn and dusk and leave the trails to them. Do not go on a trail alone, take along a dog for protection, do not remove nature's sounds with earphones, and do not leave children at the back of your group.

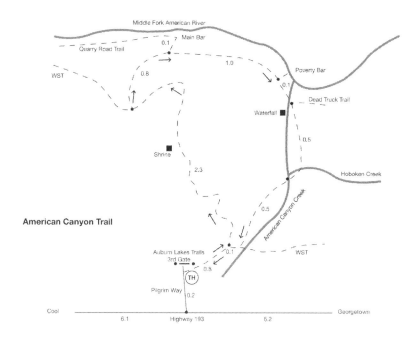

After 3.1 miles, and at the 16-mile marker, you reach another intersection. Here, you go to the right and drop down 120' to another trail junction. You want to go in the direction of Maine Bar Trail (spelled Main on maps) after stopping for a break at a small stream. Another trail takes off across the stream as part of the Western States Trail, popular with trail runners. Maine Bar is a steep, descending trail, dropping 620' over 0.8 miles. At the bottom, you reach the American Canyon Trail taking you to the right and paralleling along the Middle Fork American River. Before continuing on the main trail, you can drop down 0.1 miles to a junction with the Quarry Road Trail. You can also walk to the right down to Maine Bar at the river.

Continuing on the American Canyon Trail, you have a flat journey for the next mile. You can take a spur trail down to the river to reach Poverty Bar before returning to the American Canyon Trail. You will drop about 150' down to Poverty Bar if you choose to take this side trip. Soon after leaving the Poverty Bar area, you have a pleasant walk upstream along American Canyon Creek, lush with numerous pools and waterfalls. Then you come to a crossing of the American Canyon Creek. From this creek crossing, you start a 140' climb up to an intersection with Dead Truck Trail. Your American Canyon Trail stays to the right here (do not take the Dead Truck Trail). Immediately beyond this intersection, look for a spur trail and listen for running water. The 100' drop down this trail is well worth it, with a nice waterfall at the bottom.

Continuing along the American Canyon Trail, the path follows the creek upstream, gradually gaining in elevation over the next 0.5 miles. Next, the trail crosses Hoboken Creek and then immediately crosses American Canyon Creek again. These two creeks merge just below your crossing point. Next, you gain 345' with switchbacks to ease the climb through the forested trail over 0.5 miles. There is one more trail intersection with the Western States Trail, and you want to stay to the right here to remain on the American Canyon Trail. Soon you return to the original trail intersection, and you head to the left for the final 430' climb back to the parking area.

Share with: Joggers and equestrians (no bikes allowed).

57 – Magnolia Ranch and Greenwood Creek
Pilot Hill

Difficulty: 2
Distance: Varies depending on trail choice, but about 2.5 miles
Elevation: 50' ups and downs

Directions: On Highway 49 coming from Coloma, you will find the parking area for Magnolia Ranch on the left, 3.2 miles from the bridge crossing the South Fork American River. Coming from Auburn on Highway 49, continue 2.8 miles from Pilot Hill to the entrance on your right. Parking for cars is on the right side of the large parking area, with the remainder reserved for horse trailers.

Description: This is a fun, easy hike, with a lot of river access. There are two interlocking loops within the ranch, providing you with a variety of hiking options. The following describes just one of the possibilities.

From the parking area, walk past the service gate and start your hike in a counter-clockwise direction on Gerle Loop Trail. In about 0.25 miles, there is a fork in the trail. Continue straight here until you reach the next fork. At this fork, if you go to the right you will be on the Connector Trail taking you down to Hastings Creek, and then on into the Cronan Ranch multi-use area. Instead, go to your left here to continue on the smaller of the two loops.

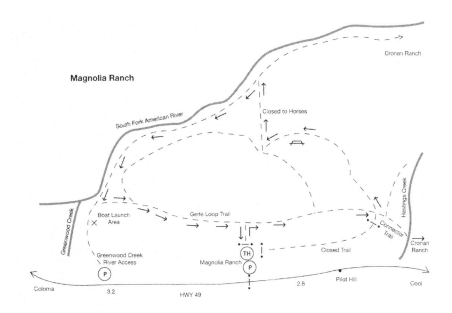

After a short uphill climb, you arrive at an area with a great view down to the river. This area also has a picnic table for a short break. Continuing with the loop, you come to a three-way intersection where the two loops meet. From here, you could pick up the larger Gerle Loop Trail again, finish the smaller loop and return to the parking area, or walk downhill on the trail marked with a sign for "No Horses."

To reach the river, take the trail to your right at this intersection (the one signed for no horse access). You walk down a steep, wide, dirt path that takes you down to the South Fork American River. At the river, you need to locate the foot trail on your left.

Along the river trail, there are numerous river access points, picnic tables, and a very interesting outdoor composting outhouse. This is a leisurely upriver walk, with spurs inviting you out to enjoy the rushing waters. Be aware that water levels can fluctuate without warnings as releases are made for the kayakers and rafters. You can put your pack down in a dry area, only to find it 15 minutes later getting wet. Never tie up your dog near the river and leave him unattended.

This portion of the trail ends at the Greenwood Creek access point where kayakers launch. From this area, find your trail heading away from the river to the left. If you continue straight here, you will end up in the parking area for Greenwood Creek. Instead, head away from the river, on a slight uphill, and rejoin the larger loop trail. Turn right onto this trail, finishing this loop back to the parking area.

Share with: Bikers and equestrians (horses have a limited access at the river, but this is a popular ride from Magnolia Ranch over to Cronan Ranch).

Less Ambitious Option: You can park at Greenwood Creek (one turn east of Magnolia Ranch) instead of Magnolia Ranch. From here, you can just take a nice stroll along the river without any elevation change. Enjoy multiple visits to the river along your walk for a truly family-friendly outing.

TRAIL INDEX

Trail	Wildflowers	Fall Colors	Waterfalls	Family Friendly	Historical	Fishing	Views	Mountain Bike	Equestrian	Snowshoe
1. El Dorado Trail				*				*	*	
2. Cronan Ranch	*			*			*	*	*	
3. Lake Clementine	*		*		*		*	*	*	
4. Hidden Falls	*		*	*			*	*	*	
5. Red Shack Trail					*					
6. Pioneer Express	*					*			*	
7. Nevada Beach		*		*	*		*			*
8. Loon Lake Snowshoe			*				*			*
9. Quarry Road	*			*	*			*	*	
10. Baldwin Beach			*				*			*
11. Dave Moore Nature Area	*			*			*			
12. South Yuba River SP	*			*	*		*			
13. Bassi Falls		*	*				*			*
14. Darrington Bike Trail	*							*		
15. Fairy Falls	*		*	*			*	*	*	
16. Feather Falls	*		*		*		*			
17. Meeks Creek & TYT		*		*		*	*		*	*
18. Van Sickle State Park	*		*				*	*		
19. TRT to Cinder Cone	*						*	*	*	
20. Caples Creek	*	*		*		*	*		*	
21. Lover's Leap	*						*			
22. Bay View Campground			*	*			*			
23. Horsetail Falls			*				*			
24. Spider & Buck Is Lakes						*	*		*	
25. Forni Lake	*						*	*	*	
26. Salmon & Loch Leven Lk	*					*	*			
27.Tamarack,Ralston,Cagwin						*	*			
28. Shealor						*	*			

*Trails 2-6 will have wildflowers in the spring

196

Trail	Wildflowers	Fall Colors	Waterfalls	Family Friendly	Historical	Fishing	Views	Mountain Bike	Equestrian	Snowshoe
29. Enchanted Pools	*		*	*		*	*	*	*	
30. Meiss Country Trails	*	*			*	*	*		*	
31. Rockbound Pass Trail	*	*				*			*	
32. Twin Lakes Trail						*				
33. Winnemucca/Round Top	*					*	*			
34. Lyons Creek	*	*		*		*	*		*	
35. Big Meadow	*						*	*	*	
36. Pearl Lake	*						*			
37. Echo Lakes Trails						*	*		*	
38. Gerle Creek			*	*		*				
39. Glen Alpine Trails			*	*			*			
40. Penner Lake	*		*			*	*	*	*	*
41. Silver Lake Trails	*		*				*	*	*	
42. Granite & Grouse Lake	*					*	*			
43. Gertrude & Tyler Lake		*				*	*			
44. Ralston Peak							*			
45. Tallac HS/Taylor Creek		*		*	*		*	*		
46. Mt. Tallac via Floating Is		*					*			
47. Lake Margaret	*	*		*		*	*			
48. Round & Bryan Meadows	*	*					*	*	*	
49. Codfish Creek Falls		*	*	*						
50. Grouse, Hemlock, Smith		*				*	*			
51. Thunder Mountain							*			
52. Eagle Lake, Vikingsholm			*	*			*			
53. Caples Lake Trails					*		*		*	
54. Confluence Trails			*		*		*			
55. Olmstead Loop Trails	*						*	*	*	
56. American Canyon Trail			*				*		*	
57. Magnolia Ranch				*		*	*	*	*	

*For wildflowers on Trails 40-55 visit earlier in the season

RESOURCES

Amador Ranger Station – El Dorado National Forest (209) 295-4251 26820 Silver Drive Pioneer, CA 95666 for information on hiking conditions along Highway 88 ((Kirkwood and Carson Pass) and the Mokelumne Wilderness
www.fs.fed.us/r5/eldorado/recreation/wild/moke/cpma

Auburn State Recreation Area (ASRA) (530) 885-4527 Office located at 501 El Dorado Street in Auburn for annual state Golden Poppy Pass. Call ahead for current office hours.

Echo Lakes (530) 659-7207 for water taxi information

El Dorado National Forest www.fs.fed.us/r5/eldorado (530) 644-6048

Folsom Lake State Recreation Area (916) 988-0205 7755 Folsom Dam Road for a map, annual state Golden Poppy Pass, and information about Folsom Lake trails like Pioneer Express Trail at Rattlesnake Bar **www.parks.ca.gov** Call ahead to verify office hours.

Foresthill Ranger District (530) 367-2224 22830 Foresthill Road **www.fs.fed.us/r5/tahoe** for information about Little Bald Mountain

Georgetown Ranger District (530-333-4312) for Hunter's Trail

Lake Tahoe Basin Management Unit (530) 543-2600 35 College Drive, South Lake Tahoe **www.fs.fed.us/r5/ltbmu**

Lake Tahoe Visitor Center 3.2 miles on Highway 89 after the 89/50 split for day permits into Desolation Wilderness

Malakoff Diggins State Historic Park (530) 265-2740 23579 North Bloomfield Road, Nevada City

Pacific Ranger District (530) 647-5415 Located on Mill Run Road in Fresh Pond off Highway 50, for trails in the Crystal Basin Recreation Area and Desolation Wilderness and to obtain Day Use Permits.

Placerville Ranger District (530) 647-5300 for information on Mormon Emigrant Trail

Tahoe National Forest (530) 265-4531 637 Coyote Street, Nevada City, CA 95959 for hikes around Nevada City

Vikingsholm (530) 525-3345 **www.parks.ca.gov/?page_id=506**

INDEX

Made in the USA
San Bernardino, CA
11 June 2019